Until Forever

Luisa Cloutier

Black Rose Writing | Texas

© Copyright 2018 by Luisa Cloutier

All rights reserved. No part of this book may be reproduced, stored in a retrieval system or transmitted in any form or by any means without the prior written permission of the publishers, except by a reviewer who may quote brief passages in a review to be printed in a newspaper, magazine or journal.

The final approval for this literary material is granted by the author.

First printing

This is a work of fiction. Names, characters, businesses, places, events and incidents are either the products of the author's imagination or used in a fictitious manner. Any resemblance to actual persons, living or dead, or actual events is purely coincidental.

ISBN: 978-1-68433-052-2
PUBLISHED BY BLACK ROSE WRITING
www.blackrosewriting.com

Printed in the United States of America
Suggested Retail Price (SRP) $17.95

Until Forever is printed in Gentium Book Basic
Cover photo and photo by Belinda Soncini

This book is a tribute to my loving husband
Brandon R. Cloutier
You will always be in my heart

Acknowledgements

Thanks to Pat who has been like a mother to me and to my mother-in-law Linda. Thanks to my friends Paula and Joe, to the manager of my fitness my studio Garrett and to all my trainers, to my Fitness Together franchise support team and to my awesome Fitness Together Northborough clients who have supported and believed in me. Thanks to my psychologist Dr. Carolyn Smith who helped me to deal with my loss and depression. And thank you Mimmo Fiorentino.

PRAISE for *Until Forever*

"Luisa Cloutier's tribute to her husband Brandon, is a beautifully written and engaging 'coming of age' journey, and the author's distinct personality and perspective are evident throughout, creating a warm and moving memoir."

–Indie Reader

"The storytelling is raw and honest."
–Nabila Fairuz, author of *The Chronicles of Captain Shelly Manhar*

"Until Forever is a story about love, loss and strength. I was drawn into the story from the first page and couldn't stop reading because I wanted to find out what happened. What struck me most about the book is Louisa's courage and determination, learning English to better communicate with a man she met and immediately felt a special connection with despite their language barrier and leaving her family in Italy to come to America with him. Life in America was a mix of happy times and struggles. Just when everything was going better than expected, it was all snatched away. Still Luisa perseveres. Her story is one of inspiration and hope."

–Diane Barnes, author of *Waiting for Ethan* and *Mixed Signals*

Until Forever

WINTER, 2014
Boylston, Massachusetts

I pull into the garage and leave the motor running. Tears blur my surroundings. I taste a salty drop flow over my lip, into my mouth. I wipe my eyes but the blurriness remains. The vibration of the huge engine of my SUV tells me what I should do. I look up at the garage door opener on the visor. So easy. Just press the button, close the door, let the exhaust fill the garage and the Escalade and eventually me. And it'll all be over.

Through the rearview mirror, I see darkness sinking outside, beginning to conceal the last of the snow in the yard and the trees, dead after the interminable winter. No one would find me for days, I'm sure. Quick, clean, over. No one would miss me. No one would care.

I wipe my eyes again and peer into the garage. In front of me, hanging from the white wall, are the two bikes that haven't moved in months. A few weeks from now, spring will be here, but I have no intention of ever riding again. Below the bikes is the yellow box of Duraflame logs, also untouched. They are supposed to be for cold March nights like tonight. But I have no interest in such things any longer. No interest in much of anything, really. It takes everything I have just to get through each day. But I am running out of steam for that too.

I look up at the garage door opener again. If only I could. Through so many difficult times in my life, my faith in God has helped me get through. But this time it only interferes. Why does God deny me doing this? Why does he do so much to hurt me, after I have believed for so long? I wish I could just dispense with a lifetime of religion and do what will take away the pain, but the doctrine is ingrained in me.

God took this option away from me too. God takes everything.

Unable to do it, I shut off the engine, silencing the SUV, then close the overhead door, sealing out the world. As I climb down out of the Escalade, I smell exhaust in the garage and hear the engine ticking as it cools. It is teasing me. My sadness becomes anger. I slam the car door shut and drag myself into the house.

The kitchen is silent. I can't stand it. I leave the lights off and drop my coat onto the counter. I can't remember the last time I cooked. I haven't eaten a bite in days and because of that I feel lightheaded, have little energy. I've become used to the dizziness when I walk, something to have with me. It is almost comforting. My throat is dry. I used to drink several liters of water a day. This week, not a drop.

As I walk into the living room, my footsteps echo off the tile floors and bare walls, reminding me of how large and empty the house is. Stairs lead to the second floor. I stop and stare through the darkness. My eyes make out the hallway upstairs. It is an open bridge to the bedroom, guarded only by the wood railing. I'm not ready to go up there yet.

I walk to the liquor cabinet and pour myself a glass of Grand Marnier. I take a sip and sink into the sofa, trying to disappear into the mute darkness.

I don't know how much time has passed. Maybe hours. I can't remember getting up and opening another bottle of wine. The one glass did plenty. The room turns around me. I close my eyes, but that makes it worse. The cause is more than the few sips of wine. My body is depleted, of food, drink, life, everything. By my intention. That isn't suicide. God can take you or let you live. That is on him.

I need to get upstairs. I think perhaps it is my time. God is taking me. But I want to go from the bedroom. I push myself up out of the sofa. My legs wobble beneath me. I am light, very little body fat. And strong. That is my profession. But my legs struggle to support me. I can hardly walk. I stagger to the stairs.

"God, please let me make it to bed," I say out loud, my voice echoing in the emptiness.

I'm not sure if I hear an answer. Maybe. I hear something. But the room is spinning. My head is in a fog. The stairs move from side to side. I grasp the railing and start to climb.

It takes forever to reach the top. I gasp for breath. I need to hold the wall for a moment not to fall. After a moment, I have the steadiness to move again. I stagger toward the bedroom door. Dizziness overwhelms me and I lose my balance. I bump into the railing and glimpse beyond it the living room floor below. I stumble backward, away from the drop, and slam into the wall behind me. I almost collapse, but somehow I manage to remain on my feet and drag myself along the wall to the bedroom.

This room is darker than the rest of the house. All of the shutters remain closed. I can't see the bed, but I know where it is. I head in that direction. The dizziness intensifies. I collapse onto the bed. I feel a strange sensation, as though my body is separating from my soul. God is taking me.

"I'm ready," I say out loud.

I have almost no strength left. The dizziness has become a noise in my head, a deafening cacophony. I squeeze my temples. It is painful.

"Take me, God," I shout.

Relief. Salvation. I hope in desperation.

"God, is this my time?" I call out.

Through the noise in my head and the darkness surrounding me, I hear his voice. Yes...

I start crying, thankful that it is finally happening.

PART ONE

CHAPTER 1

For most of my early life, mornings were always the same. We woke up in the morning to the hiss of the espresso machine as my mom made coffee. The smell welcomed us to the kitchen where we found warm bread and a jar of Nutella waiting at the table. Sometimes my mom had freshly baked cookies. She always made sure we ate well and left happy.

There were four of us. My older brother Paolo, who used to pick on me when he wasn't chasing the neighborhood girls. The older he got, the more interest he had in them and the less in annoying me. I was the second oldest. I had one sister, Angela, who was three years younger than I, and another brother, Rodolfo, five years younger than I. For my mom, we were her life.

After she made sure we all had breakfast, she would start cooking the ragù, the meat and tomato sauce that we put on pasta for most of our meals. The ragù would cook for hours, filling every room with the smell of garlic and basil and wine. While it simmered on the stove, she cleaned the apartment and then made lunch, usually a salad and a side dish, like *melanzane a funghetti*, the sautéed eggplant that my father loved. At 1:00pm the whole family would come home and eat a huge meal together, and then we would all go back to school. My mother spoiled us.

For years she begged my father to let her get her driver's license. In those days in Italy, wives were expected to get their husband's permission for things like that. He didn't agree until she was almost thirty. It took another eight years for him to buy her a car, a Fiat 126, a tiny, boxy, very popular car in those days. It looked a bit like the modern Cooper Mini, but even smaller. My mom was thrilled with it.

She got the car around the time I finished high school. I found a job at a construction company in town, but since I was only seventeen, I still didn't have my driver's license so my mom offered to drive me to work every morning in her prized car. The road was bad, dotted with pot holes that sent her little Fiat bouncing up and down so much I thought the car and the two of us were going to fall apart.

My job required me to be the first to arrive each morning to open the office. Having my mom drive me meant I didn't have to leave so early. She seemed to like the extra time with me, too.

"Are things getting better at work?" she asked me this morning.

"The boss is good at getting people to lend him money to build, but he doesn't seem to know how to pay it back when it's due. I think a couple of people are chasing him for their money. He hides a lot."

"Oh, my God. You be careful, Luisa."

"Nothing is going to happen to me. I'm just worried that my paycheck is going to bounce one day."

"Just don't get involved in his business problems, you understand?" my mother said.

"I need to find a different job."

"Why don't you get married? You and Nino should start a family and then you won't have to work like this."

"I'm not going to start a family with a cheater."

"You haven't forgiven him?" my mother asked.

"No."

"He's a good man," she told me. "He made a mistake."

"He knew what he was doing."

"I'm sure he's sorry."

"How's he going to have sex with his boss's daughter, and then argue with me when I say he has to leave that job? How can I trust him? He still looks at other girls."

"Italian men are like that. It doesn't mean anything. He knows that you're watching him now. He'll behave himself. He's not a bad man, Luisa. He works hard. He goes to church. He's from a good family. I think he'll make a good husband. You'll see. Once you two have your own children, he'll be different."

"I'm not interested in having children right now. And definitely not with Nino."

"What are you talking about? Why not?"

"I'm not you, Mamma. I want to do other things first. I don't want to stay here in Napoli my whole life. I want to see other places."

"Have you talked about this with Nino?"

"I don't have to talk about it with Nino. He doesn't own me. He acts like he does, but he doesn't. He hasn't even asked me to marry him."

"He will. You don't date a girl for two years and not get married."

"You don't date a girl for two years and go sleep with your boss's daughter, either."

We reached the construction company office, and she pulled in front.

"You do what you think is best, Luisa," she said, "but I think you should give him a chance."

"How many chances does he get?"

She reached over and put her hand on mine.

"You have to follow your heart," she said. "Look into your heart and you'll know what to do."

· · · · ·

One Friday I was preparing the payroll as usual at the construction company. Two carpenters stood by the door, waiting for their checks. Everyone had been worried that this was the week the boss wouldn't pay them. So far, he had only stiffed the lenders, but we all knew it was just a matter of time.

The phone on my desk rang. "Luisa, is that you?" she asked. I recognized the voice of Roberta Ombre, the neighbor in the apartment below ours. She was breathing heavily, rushing her words.

"What's wrong, Mrs. Roberta?"

"It's your mother," she said.

· · · · ·

One of the carpenters drove me to the hospital in Pozzuoli, where my mother had been taken. I ran into the emergency room and saw my sister

Angela in the waiting room, crying. She jumped up when she saw me.

"Oh, my God, Luisa."

"What happened? How is she? Where's Mamma?"

"She was dead!" Angela said.

"What? No!"

I turned to go find her, but Angela grabbed me by the shoulders.

"They said she was dead and they couldn't do anything but I begged her to wake up and all of a sudden her heart started beating again and she opened her eyes and the doctors said God felt sorry for me and let Mamma live and now...!"

"What are you talking about?" This made no sense to me. "Where's Mamma?" I started toward the doorway to the treatment area.

Angela hurried behind me. "She's going to be okay, they said. She's going to live."

I just needed to see her. I rushed into the treatment area. A nurse took me to my mother's bed. The moment I saw her there in the bed, with tubes and IV's and monitors attached, I nearly cried. But I held it in and barely heard the doctor explain that my mother had a flu, nothing more. They only thing that mattered was that he said she was going to be all right and they were sending her home.

. . . . .

That evening, I sat with my mother in her bedroom. My father was in the kitchen eating with the others. We were taking turns looking after her. My mother asked me to close the door. She wanted to talk to me.

When I sat back down, she said, "Listen to me, Luisa. This is important."

"What is it, mamma?"

"If anything happens to me..."

I didn't want to hear that. "Nothing's going to happen to you," I said.

She shushed me and said, "Let me finish. If anything happens to me, you know what you have to do."

I wasn't sure what she meant, and I didn't want to know. "Nothing's going to happen to you, mamma. The doctor said it's a flu. You're going to be all right."

"This time, I know. But if something ever happens..."

"Mamma, please. The thing is, you do too much. You're always working around here, doing everything. Cooking. Cleaning. Taking me to work. Washing the clothes. Buying the food. It's too much. You need to rest. That's all that's the matter. You've been doing too much."

"Luisa, please, listen to me."

"We'll take care of things, Mamma, don't worry. We'll help you from now on. Things will be better, you'll see."

"If something happens to me," she said again.

"Mamma—"

"Listen to me. If something happens, you have to take care of the family. You understand?"

"Stop worrying about that. Nothing's going to happen to you."

"You understand what I'm asking you, Luisa?" She strained to push herself up off the bed a few inches. "Please," she said, "tell me you understand."

"Of course I understand, but nothing is going to happen to you."

My mom sank back down on the bed, looking a little relieved. But there was still a darkness in her expression. "I asked God one wish," she said.

"Why are you talking like this?"

"I ask that when it's my time to go..."

"Mamma, please."

"...not to let my kids see me die."

"For God's sake, stop!" I said.

But she didn't. "Have people from the neighborhood find me, take care of things, so my children don't have to see."

"Stop saying that!"

My father must have heard me raise my voice because I heard footsteps in the hallway, and the door flew open and he rushed in.

"What's going on in here? Lina, are you all right?"

I spun around toward him, angry. "It's your fault!"

"What?"

"You make her work so hard."

"What are you talking about?" he said.

My mother grasped my hand and said, "Luisa, be quiet."

I wasn't listening. I pulled my hand free and took a step toward my father. "If anything happens to her, I'm going to kill you!"

"Luisa!" my mother said, pushing herself up a few inches. "Stop it."

My father stared at me, too shocked to answer.

A week later, I was at work, answering the phone as I always did, when my older brother called and said the ambulance had taken my mother to the hospital again and I should come.

"Hurry," Paolo said.

When I got there, I found Paolo sitting alone in the hallway, his head bent over, resting in his hands.

I hurried toward him, saying, "Paolo!"

He looked up, and I saw that he was crying. He didn't have to say a word. I knew from the look on his face that Mamma was dead.

"Noooo!" I screamed. The rest is a blur, but I know that several nurses and doctors held me down. I don't know what they gave me, but whatever it was, it was the only thing that could calm me.

My father came from work and drove us all home from the hospital, leaving my mother's body there. He said it would be taken care of. I didn't see him cry when he stood beside her before leaving her for the last time, but I was sure that he was being strong for the rest of us. He had to be as shattered as we were.

When we got home, the house smelled of the ragù my mother had made earlier in the day after she had returned from dropping me off at work. I walked to her bedroom door and just stared at the bed for I don't know how long, realizing that she wasn't going to return, ever. The words she had spoken from there just a week ago reverberated in my memory. She'd be worried about who was going to take care of the family. She'd begged me to do it. Her dying wish...

"Luisa," my father called out from down the hall.

I walked toward his voice and found him and my brothers and sister sitting in the kitchen. He looked up at me, waiting.

"What, papa?" I said.

"We have to eat something."

I struggled to breathe. "I'm not hungry right now," I said.

He looked surprised. At first I thought he was concerned about me, but then he said, "The rest of us have to eat something."

He stared again, waiting for me to bring lunch.

Still too stunned to react, I trudged across the kitchen to the refrigerator, not knowing what I was going to do about lunch or anything else. I opened the refrigerator and saw the large dish my mother always put the raw meatballs in. She'd prepared everything, seasoned them and stuffed them with mozzarella, but she hadn't fried them, expecting to be here right now to do the cooking.

The devastation came over me so suddenly I wasn't prepared. My legs gave out beneath me and I collapsed to the floor. I started to cry. Through my wailing, I heard my father's voice.

"Luisa. Luisa!"

I turned my head, still weeping, and looked at him for comfort, sure he would come over and hold me, tell me that everything was going to be all right.

"Let's go, Luisa," he said. "The kids are hungry." He gestured with his chin toward the dish of meatballs in the refrigerator. "We have to eat," he said.

I looked at my brothers and my sister staring down at me, my father waiting. He turned and peered into the refrigerator. I knew what I had to do. I wiped the tears from my face and pushed myself to my feet. Taking the dish of meatballs over to the stove, I filled a skillet with olive oil and began to fry them.

"Take care of the family," my mother had told me. I could not let her down.

CHAPTER 2

I had seen how much work my mother did for the family, but I didn't fully realize the extent of it all until everything fell on me to do.

With my mother gone, someone had to prepare breakfast, lunch and dinner for my father and my brothers and sister, seven days a week. Someone had to clean the apartment, wash the clothes, hang them on the line, iron my father's dress shirts and then iron all of the bed sheets. Someone had to go to the different markets to buy food, deal with my youngest brother Rodolfo's school, drop Angela off at her work. The list never ended. It was a full time job.

I had to leave the construction company.

On top of all the work, someone had to be the support for Angela and Rodolfo, who were younger than I was, so they were struggling even more with the loss of their mother.

Only a few nights after we buried my mother, I walked past Rodolfo's room and heard weeping. It was late, I was tired, and I didn't have the strength to deal with that right then. But I knew that if I felt this bad, imagine how he was feeling. What would my mom have done? What did she expect me to do? I knew the answer.

I tapped on Rodolfo's door. When he didn't answer, I inched it open. Light from the hall behind me cut into the darkness of his room. I saw him in bed, tears soaking his face and the pillowcase.

"What's the matter?" I asked, though I knew the answer. We all missed my mom and couldn't imagine going on without her.

"I want to sleep with Mamma," he said.

"It's going to be all right," I told him. "It takes time, but everything's going to be okay."

I didn't believe the words myself. How could he?

He shook his head and kept crying. "I miss her."

I came in and closed the door, sealing out the light. The dim glow from the streetlights gave the room a sad grayness.

"We all miss her, Rodolfo," I whispered.

He didn't answer, just wept.

I walked to the bed, and bent down and stroked his hair. "Mamma's watching us from heaven," I said. "She'll make sure we're all right."

"I want her to be here, not in heaven."

So did I. But what could I say? He continued to weep. Even though I had no more words to tell him that would make him feel better, I couldn't leave him like this, so I lay in bed on top of the covers and held him until his weeping faded away and he drifted off to sleep. When I knew he wouldn't wake up, I left and went to my own bed. There, alone, it felt as gray and dismal as Rodolfo's had been, but I had no one to hold me and comfort me and remind me that everything would be all right.

Earlier, I had tried to call Nino but couldn't reach him. Maybe tomorrow we could be together and he could give me the strength I tried to give Rodolfo and the rest of my family. As I lay in bed, I kept telling myself that with time, things would get better.

But things didn't get better. In fact, they got worse.

My father quickly got used to my doing many of the things that my mom had done around the house and he began expecting more. If he came home from work when I was at the fruit market or the butcher shop or picking up his suits at the dry cleaners, he would question me about where I was, looking annoyed, as though my not being home was something against him. It was almost as though he never wanted me to leave the house.

Maybe this is why I never went out, to do something for me. I didn't want to hurt him. That, along with being sad that mom was gone, and tired with all the work I had to do around the house.

Nino was no support. He took a job in Brescia, in the north of Italy, only coming down to Giugliano every few months for a day or two. I rarely saw him when he was here, and when he did come over to the house, we never did anything together. We sat in the kitchen or living room, talked a little, never really alone, never able to get close. It was like I was still by myself. Sometimes he brought his laundry for me to do, and I guess I was so used to doing everything for everyone that I did it. Then he'd go back to Brescia.

He hardly ever called. He always had an excuse, too busy, the phone weren't working, he wasn't feeling well. I couldn't help but wonder what the real reason was. Mamma had said that he was a good man and he loved me, but I could never make peace with his lack of faithfulness, even if that was what all Italian men did. Maybe I wasn't meant to be with an Italian man. Sometimes it seemed that maybe I wasn't meant to be with anyone at all. Nino made it easy to think that way.

I forgot him most of the time because the problems at home occupied much of my thought. Rodolfo began staying out late from time to time. When he did, I always waited up in my bed until I heard the key in the door and Rodolfo coming in. Only then could I fall asleep. If I questioned him too much or pushed too hard for him not to stay out so late, he would say, "You're not my mother," and walk away angry.

Angela, too, began staying out late. I would see her leave the apartment in short, tight dresses and high heels.

"Where did you get those clothes?" I asked. "And where are you going?"

"Come on, Luisa, where do you think I'm going?" she said. "It's Saturday night. There's a new club near Lido."

"Does papa know?"

"I'm eighteen. Eighteen year olds go out on Saturday. Twenty-one year olds do too," she said. "Why don't you come? We'll dance. Meet boys. It'll be fun."

"No, I can't."

"Why not?"

"I can't. I have things to do."

She shrugged. "Suit yourself."

"Be careful," I told her. "Boys put drugs in girls' drinks so they can take advantage of them."

"I'm just going to dance, Luisa. Stop worrying."

But I did worry. I worried the way I knew Mamma would have worried if she were here.

Christmas was filled with memories of my mother. Just getting through it and helping my family cope took all the strength I had. The rest of the winter wore me down. By the time spring arrived, I was so deep in my depression that I couldn't imagine ever getting out of it.

With summer came the phone call from Nino. He said he was moving back Guigliano. Maybe things would get better having him nearby, I thought. Maybe we could rebuild the relationship. The long winter without him, at the time I had needed him most, had left me bitter, but I tried to keep in mind what my mother had said, that he was a good man and he loved me.

"What are you going to do for work?" I asked. He'd gone to Brescia because of the job there.

"I'll be okay."

"Do you have a job? I can ask my father if he knows of anything."

"I'm okay, Luisa." He tried to change the subject, talking about the friend who was going to let him share the apartment, but I didn't just drop it. I had my suspicions.

"What does that mean, Nino? Do you have a job or don't you?"

"Yes. I told you. So forget..."

"Where?" I asked.

He mumbled his answer.

I wanted to strangle him. I had a pretty idea what he was saying. "Where are you going to work, Nino?"

He hesitated, then finally sighed and said, "Lido Varca d'oro."

"No," I said. That was where he had cheated with his boss's daughter. "I'm not going to go through this again," I said.

"Come on, Luisa."

"If you go back to work there, I'm done with you."

"What are you talking about? Why are you saying that?"

"Why?" I said. I couldn't believe he was asking me why.

"I need to work, Luisa."

"Work with your father at his construction business."

"He doesn't have any openings, and I don't do that kind of work. It'll be all right at the Lido, I promise you."

"It's disrespectful to me."

"No it isn't. You have it all wrong."

"If you go to work there again, we're done. Period." I hung up.

. . . . .

A week later, on a Sunday afternoon, while I was ironing my father's shirts, the front buzzer rang. I could hear the monotonous murmur of the Formula 1 race my father was watching on television.

"Can you answer that, Papa?" I said.

He didn't respond.

The buzzer rang again.

"Papa?"

"Get that, Luisa, will you?" he called out.

There was no use arguing. I left the ironing and walked through the living room toward the door. "You could get that, Papa. I'm working."

He gestured toward the TV without looking at me.

When I opened the door, I found Nino standing outside, clutching a bouquet of red roses the size of the Colosseum.

"Nino!"

I was so happy to see him, and so happy that he remembered how much I loved roses and that he took the time to get them for me.

"You see," he said, "I came back. I couldn't bear to be away from you any longer."

I wanted to jump into his arms, but I had to ask him first. I had to make sure.

"You changed your mind?" I said.

"No." He grinned. "I told you I was coming back and here I am."

"I mean about working at the Lido Varca D'Oro. Did you change your mind?"

His smile disappeared. "Luisa, you haven't seen me in months and that's how you...?"

I held up my hand to stop him.

"Nino, are you going to work there or not?"

He lowered his eyes.

I knew his answer before he even said it.

"Then we're done," I said. "And I don't want your roses."

"Come on, Luisa. Stop that. Take the roses."

"I told you."

"And I have to work. A man has to work. You have to trust me."

"We're done," I said again and closed the door on him.

He knocked on the door.

"Luisa!" he called out.

I didn't answer.

"Fine. Suit yourself," he said.

I stood at the door, listening to his footsteps stomping away as he descended the stairs and left the building.

"Was that Nino?" my father said.

I went in and told him what had happened.

"Are you crazy?" he said. "The man needs a job. You can't tell him take this job, don't take that job. What are you doing?"

"No, Papa."

"Go get him."

"No, I'm not going to stand for this anymore."

"Stand for what?"

"You know what he did."

"That was before. Think, Luisa!" he said, poking his forehead. "You're not young. You don't think everyone knows you've been with him. Who's going to marry you? You...you...you're damaged goods."

"Papa!" I jumped up, clenching my teeth so he wouldn't see me cry.

"You know what I mean. This is a small town. You know how people think."

I stormed away to my room and closed the door, hating Nino, hating this "small town," hating my father's way of thinking, and hating myself for having let Nino get away with treating me like that for so long. But most of all, I hated that everything my father said was probably the truth.

The next morning I was outside on the balcony, hanging the clothes on the line strung across the road. I looked down and saw Nino peddling up the street on his bike. He was dressed in the white shorts and white shirt that was the uniform of workers at the Lido Varca D'Oro.

He looked up at me and waved. I didn't move. He was certain I would forgive him. It was only a matter of time. I'd forgiven so much more already. But this morning, seeing the look on his face, watching him heading off to the Lido Varca D'Oro, I was left with a real pain in my throat and nausea bubbling up from my stomach. That one thing he wouldn't do for me. He'd left me alone after my mother died, left me alone over the holidays and in the dead of winter.

He didn't love me. My mother was wrong about that.

That night, as I went to bed, I prayed to God to send me a good man, a man I could trust, a man who would love me, a man who would take me far away from this place and protect me and give me a good life, a life nothing like the one I was living, nothing like the life my mother had had.

CHAPTER 3

A few months after I broke up with Nino, I was in the kitchen with Angela, slicing zucchini for that night's dinner. She sat at the table, telling me about her day at work. Hearing her stories, I missed the days when I used to leave the apartment for work. As bad as things had been there, with people chasing my boss for money, at least I saw people, I did things. I had a life. Now it seemed I cooked and cleaned most of the time, only leaving to run errands. If I could have changed things, I would have, but I was stuck.

Rodolfo's girlfriend Rita arrived. Rodolfo wasn't home yet so she joined Angela at the kitchen table.

"Did you hear about the dance?" she asked.

"What dance?" Angela asked.

"The American Marines, they're having a dance this weekend, in Villagio Coppola, at Ten Downy."

"God, I love American Marines. They're so sexy."

"So let's go, okay?" Rita said.

"Definitely." Angela turned to me. "Luisa?"

"Go, but be careful. Come home before…"

"No, you come too."

"Me?" I laughed. "No thanks."

Rita came over to the counter where I was chopping vegetables. "You're a free woman now, Luisa. Go get yourself a Marine."

I laughed and felt myself blush. "I'm too old for those things."

Angela came over too and stood on the other side of me.

"No, you're not, Luisa. You're only three years older than me."

"Three years is a long time," I said. "Besides, I don't speak English."

"None of us do. Dancing is international. You don't have to speak English to dance. And I know you like to dance."

"You go," I said. "Forget about me this time. Maybe the next one."

"No, you're going to come," Angela said. She turned to Rita. "We're all going, the three of us. No, four of us. We'll see if cousin Rosalia wants to come, too."

"And Elena," Rita said.

"Good idea, her too. This will be great!"

"You can all go," I said. "But not me. I'm not going."

"We're all going," Angela repeated.

"It'll be good for you," Rita told me.

"Listen..." I started to say.

Speaking at the same time, both Angela and Rita said, "You're going!"

The idea of going there terrified me, but inside I thought maybe they were right, maybe it would be good for me to get out. I wasn't going to dance with anyone, but maybe it would be good to go and listen to the music, just get out of the house for a change.

I shrugged and said, "What would I wear?"

"Let's go pick something," Angela said. "You've got a great body. We're going to make sure you show it off."

She and Rita rushed up the hallway toward my room, giggling. I couldn't help but laugh too. Nervous laughter. I hurried up the hallway after them. I was scared of the idea of going, but part of me understood that maybe it was a good idea. Every time I didn't want to do something and yet I ended up doing it, it usually turned out to be the right thing to do. Perhaps this was like that. I hoped it was, anyway.

The club was packed. Loud music blasted out the doors and into the parking lot. As we walked toward the door in our high heels, I noticed a young couple off to the side, trying to hide in the shadows, kissing. I thought of Nino. I thought of how lonely I was, not only now, but also when I was with Nino. I thought of how it might feel to be with a man who I really loved and who really loved me back.

I would find that love someday, I reminded myself. I was always a dreamer, even when life showed me little more than nightmares. But whatever the bleakness that surrounded me, I never let go of my dreams.

Inside the club the music was so loud we could barely talk to each other. It was mostly American hip hop and techno club pop, heavily synthesized with a contagious beat that drove you to move your body. The dance floor was crowded with bodies pulsating to the music, everyone bumping into each other, everyone looking so young to me. You could tell the American Marines. Most with short blond hair. Or black skin and no hair. The Italian girls went crazy for them.

"Let's dance!" Angela yelled and grabbed my hand, pulling me toward the dance floor.

I pulled away. "You go. I'm not ready."

I don't think she heard what I said, but she seemed to get the message. She and Elena started dancing together. Rita and Rosalia disappeared into the crowd. I found a table off to the side and ordered a Campari. The music itself was great, the driving beat so loud that for a while I didn't think about anything outside the club. Being here made me feel young again, almost carefree.

The rest of the girls came and joined me eventually, had some drinks, disappeared back onto the dance floor. They flirted with guys, even though some of them had boyfriends. I decided it was all for fun. I wished I could be that free. But even though it felt good to be here, I was quiet. And I had always been a little shy, never good at flirting and going up to men I didn't know.

Much of the time I was by myself. Still, I told myself it was good that I was here. I enjoyed just listening to the music and watching the people.

Half an hour after we arrived, the music changed from hip hop to a slow ballad. Bryan Adams' sang, "Everything I do, I do it for you." I really liked that song so when it came on, I closed my eyes and...

"Hi. Excuse me."

The man's voice snapped my attention. I opened my eyes and saw an American Marine standing in front of me. He was tall, with eyes the color of the water in the Blue Grotto. The overalls and the white t-shirt he wore barely covered his muscular arms and shoulders. The first thought that flashed into my head was how good it must feel to be held by this man.

Angela or one of the others must have returned to the table without me noticing, which was why he was here, I thought. So I glanced around to see who he came to talk to. I was the only one there. But I saw Angela and the others coming this way from the bar. Angela looked shocked. The others giggled and pointed at me.

"Hi," the American Marine said again, drawing my attention back to him. "Ma'am, would you like to dance with me?" he asked.

I wasn't sure I heard him right. I understood enough English to know what he was asking, but it didn't make sense. I made a vague gesture, pointing to myself, and gave him a questioning look.

"Yes, you," he said. "You're beautiful. I would love to dance with you."

All I could do was shake my head "no."

Undeterred, he reached down and took my hand. I was struck by the size of his hand, large and strong. He could have crushed my hand, but he held me gently, carefully and said, "Please. Dance with me tonight."

I couldn't understand why he was asking me, why he'd come over to me. There were so many beautiful girls in this place. Why me? Angela and Rita had a good time helping me dress nicely to come here, but I knew I wasn't beautiful, not like so many of the other girls there.

"No. Thank you," I said.

By now Angela and the others had reached the table and told me in Italian to go dance.

"Hi," the Marine said to the others.

They all said "Hiiiiii" in that flirting way they had, giggling. The Marine nodded and turned back to me.

"Please," he said. "Dance with me. Please."

"*Si vai balla!*" they all yelled at me, telling me to dance. Angela came around behind me and practically pushed me out of the chair. She whispered in my ear that he was gorgeous, was I insane, go dance with him.

Between his alluring eyes and manner and the others practically forcing me to go, I got up, took his strong hand and walked out to the dance floor with him.

With Bryan Adams playing, the craziness of the dance floor had changed to a sea of couples locked in embrace, swaying with the melody of the song. He put his arms around me. He felt so solid and strong. My body shuddered for an instant, something I couldn't control.

"Is everything okay?" he asked.

I understood the word "okay?" and nodded.

He took control of my body as we danced. Even though it was a slow dance, the way he held me and led me, I felt for that brief moment like I belonged to him. The scent of his body overtook my senses. It wasn't cologne. It was just him. I closed my eyes and let his essence and his strength and the music take me.

"You're a good dancer," he said into my ear. "Do you like this song?"

I nodded. I wished I could speak more English. But even if I could, I was so nervous at that moment I probably wouldn't have been able to speak anyway.

It had taken me so long to say yes to dancing with him that the song ended too quickly. When it was done, he took a step back and looked into my eyes again.

"Grazie for the dance, ma'am," he said.

"*Prego*," I said. Again I didn't know what to say. I didn't know how to flirt in English. I wasn't even good at it in Italian. I wished the dance hadn't ended, but now that it was over, I found myself standing awkwardly in front of him, staring. The music switched back to hip hop. Bodies flooded the dance floor, bumping into both of us.

It was really over. I turned and rushed back to the table where Angela and the others were watching us and smiling.

"What happened?" Angela asked. "Why did you walk away? Go back and dance more with him."

I glanced behind me, thinking that was what I really wanted to do, but I saw that he was gone, disappeared into the crowd, probably dancing with a younger, prettier girl. He hadn't liked dancing with me. He didn't like me. Probably when he'd come over to ask me before, because of the poor light he hadn't gotten a good look. He'd been disappointed, but he probably just went through with the dance to be polite. The American Marines were always polite.

"Oh, my God, Luisa," Angela said, pulling me into the chair next to her. "Tell me everything. Who is he? Where did he come from?"

"I don't know. He's American."

"I know he's American. He's also like the most gorgeous guy in the place. What's his name?"

"I don't know."

"You didn't ask?"

"I forgot to ask."

"Are you crazy?"

I had been so nervous when he came over, I hadn't been thinking straight. But he hadn't asked my name either, so I was certain he wasn't interested. He was just being polite, after all. He was gorgeous, though. My sister was right about that. I had never in my life seen a man as handsome he was. Men like that didn't date girls like me.

"Did you see the way he looked at you?" Angela asked.

"He didn't look at me in any way," I said.

"Are you blind?" Rita said. "He couldn't keep his eyes off your body."

"Or his hands," Elena said. "Did you see how he held her?"

"How did it feel, those arms around you?" Rosalia asked.

It had felt like heaven, but I answered with a shrug and said, "Okay," as if it were no big deal. I had always kept my feelings private. The last thing I would ever do was tell them, or anyone else, how I really felt.

What I really felt was a strange mixture of happiness at how good it had felt to dance with such a good-looking man, but sadness that now it was over, he was gone and I didn't even know his name. Though I knew I'd never see him again, the few minutes on the dance floor with him started me thinking that maybe I wasn't as ugly as I had always believed I was. I remembered the day I'd overheard my mother and Gianna talking about me "growing into my looks." Maybe I really was.

CHAPTER 4

A week after I let Angela and Rita convince me to go the dance, I let them convince me to go back to Ten Downy again. There wasn't a dance this night, but I went in hopes of seeing the Marine who had danced with me. I hadn't stopped thinking about him since that night. And I'd had a taste of what it was like to be alive and free again, and I wanted more.

I made sure to have dinner ready for my father before I went out, but he still didn't seem to like it.

"What are you going to do there?" he said. He didn't question Angela. Just me.

"Everything's done in the house. I want to go out and have a little fun, Papa."

Angela came up beside me. "She's looking for her American fantasy man."

"No, I'm not."

My father glowered at me. "Stay away from the Americans."

"What's wrong with the Americans?" I asked. "Mama always said that they helped us in World War Two, that they were good protectors, that…"

"Your mother married an Italian, not an American. That should tell you something."

"Papa, I'm just going to go out for a few hours and have a little fun," I said. "I work hard. I deserve a little play too. I'm not marrying anybody tonight, all right?"

"Funny. Take care of your little sister," he told me. "And I want you home early."

Angela kissed him on the cheek. "We'll try not wake you up when we come in." She giggled, teasing him.

"I'll be waiting."

· · · · ·

When we arrived at the club, there were many more Marines than Italians. Angela and I started toward the bar to order drinks. We walked past the part of the club with pool tables and other games. I had only taken a few steps when I saw him, leaning over a pool table, lining up his shot.

His eyes followed the pool stick, past the white ball, and up to where I was standing. He didn't move. He remained leaning, in mid shot, not taking the shot, not getting up, just frozen there, staring at me. Our eyes locked. I couldn't move either. I felt myself blush and managed a nervous smile. His lips bent into a smile, and for an instant I saw that same look of captivation, of desire, that I had seen a week ago.

He slid the stick and the balls clattered around the table, the sound jarring me back into reality. I noticed now that Angela had continued to the bar and I realized I was standing alone, which unnerved me. I don't know what came over me, but I had to get away. I hurried to the bar to join my sister. My legs were shaking.

"Angela, I saw him."

"He's here?" She peered past me, trying to spot him. "Where?"

I pointed. "What do I do?"

She saw him and nodded. "Okay, follow me."

"What do you mean? What do I do?"

"I know what to do."

She took my hand and forced me to walk with her as she headed back where we had come from and over to the pool tables. When I realized what she was doing, I pulled her to try to stop her.

"No, no," I said. "I can't."

"Just let me take care of this. I know what I'm doing."

She practically pulled me all the way to the pool table where the Marine was playing. He looked up when we approached, first at Angela, who was in front, but he quickly looked directly at me and held his stare. I felt shy and looked down.

"Hi," Angela said to him.

"Hello."

"I'm Angela. This is my sister, Luisa."

"I'm Brandon. It's nice to meet you." He shook Angela's hand and then he reached over and shook mine. "Nice to meet you, Luisa."

The feel of his hand again brought back memories of the previous week. A shiver ran up my spine. I was too embarrassed to say anything. Walking up to someone like this was something Angela could pull off. I couldn't.

"Okay," Angela said. "Brandon, would you like to speak to my sister?"

"Yes, sure."

"Okay. Here she is." She pulled me forward, right in front of him, and said, "I have to go." Then she walked away, leaving me alone with Brandon.

I wanted to kill her.

. . . . .

We sat and talked in spite of my nervousness and our language barrier. I had studied English in school, but only remembered a few words. His Italian was limited, but better than my English. We could say basic, simple sentences, but that was about it.

"How old you are?" I asked. He looked very young. My father had always told me that the husband should always be at least four or five years older than the wife, like Nino was with me.

"You first," Brandon said.

"I have twenty-three."

He smiled. "I have twenty-three, too."

"You tease my English?"

"No way. It's much better than my Italian."

My father wasn't going to like that he was only twenty-three. But he seemed more mature than that. If this ever went anywhere, my father would see that and it would be all right.

Brandon reached over and gently took hold of my gold necklace. "I like this," he said. "Where did you get it?"

"In Napoli."

"It's nice."

"You like?"

"Yes, I like. I'm going to go to Naples and get one for myself."

"Good for you."

"How am I going to find the place?" he said. "I guess you'll have to take me there, show me where it is."

I smiled and held in my laughter. That was such an obvious line. Americans were so different from Italian men. An Italian man would have had his hands all over me. The Americans played it coy. I didn't mind though. It meant Brandon was interested in me. That still surprised me, but it made me feel happy.

"I take you," I said.

"So then you'll have to give me your phone number so I can call you."

This time I laughed out loud.

. . . . .

We went to Naples a few days later. After that we went to the swimming pool at Corney Park together. Some friends of mine were there and I introduced him to them. Everyone liked him right away. He started holding my hand. He had a white Alpha Romeo sports car, and when he picked me up in it and we drove to Naples, I felt like everyone was looking at us, envying me.

We loved to walk near the sea together. Brandon always held my hand and told me stories about America. I only understood a little of what he was saying, but what I did understand fascinated me. I always dreamed of visiting other places in the world. Talking with Brandon was almost like going away from Naples for a brief moment.

Communicating was always difficult, but we tried and laughed and seemed to do okay. That first day he took me for a Margherita pizza and gelato. Afterward, anything I wanted he would say buy it. He'd say, don't worry about it, he'd take care of it. He paid for everything, a big change from Nino, who was always short of money. And he was always polite and attentive. With him, I knew I was well-taken-care-of and protected.

And respected. Days passed and he didn't even try to kiss me. Then two weeks. Then three... I felt closer to him. I experienced a strange connection to his body even though we had done nothing more intimate than holding hands and hugging. But there was a special connection. He was the kind of man I had always dreamed about, nothing at all like Nino, or my father, or anyone else I knew in Italy.

Wanting to get closer, I tried to learn English. He struggled to memorize more words in Italian. We were together most nights. We drove to Naples a lot, too. It was exciting being in the city with him. Sometimes we went dancing. He usually took me to dinner. Other times we just walked together, barely speaking. My life, which had been sad for so long, had changed abruptly when I met Brandon. Sometimes I wasn't sure it was really happening. I was also afraid that it would not last.

One night when we were driving back from Naples in my mother's Fiat because Brandon's car wasn't working, a car on the opposite side of the road flashed its headlights at us as we approached. It was well past midnight on a road that usually wasn't busy at this hour.

"What that is?" I said.

Brandon slowed down. "You think someone is in trouble?" he said. "Maybe they need help."

We drew closer, moving slowly now. Just as Brandon brought the car to a stop and began to roll down the window, I recognized whose car it was. It was too late to stop him. I shivered in the chilly air that came through the window, fearing what was going to happen between them.

"Is everything okay?" Brandon said out the window.

I moved so I could see past Brandon and into the car stopped alongside us. Both cars were blocking the road, but no one else came from either direction.

"*Come stai, Luisa?*" Nino said. He looked between me and Brandon. I could tell from his eyes that he was up to no good.

Brandon looked at me. "You know him?"

Before I could answer, Nino gestured toward Brandon and said to me, "*Il tuo nuovo salsiccia?*"

I couldn't believe he was calling Brandon that. He wouldn't be so brave if he thought Brandon understood him. I didn't know what Brandon would do if he did know that Nino had called him a sausage, a slang for boyfriend, so instead of telling him I sneered at Nino and said, "*Stai zitto!*" hoping he would shut up.

Nino just laughed.

I looked at Brandon. "We go, *si?*"

"Of course, Luisa. Just one second."

Brandon turned and glared at Nino. I could see his reflection in the mirror. His eyes were fierce and never veered from Nino. His jaw showed that he had clenched his teeth. He held his lips tightly, as if a firestorm of words was about to leap out at Nino and it was taking all his strength to hold back. He exuded strength. Nino tried to stare back, but he only lasted for a moment. Then his eyes lowered and he turned his head.

"*Ciao,*" Brandon said, and I'd never before heard that word uttered as a threat, but this time I saw how that single word from Brandon filled Nino with fear. Nino rolled up his window and drove away.

Brandon turned back to me. "Don't worry about him," he said. "You're with me now."

In that moment I knew for sure that my feelings for him were real, that he was the right man for me, that with him I would always be protected and taken care of.

· · · · ·

I arrived home late and found Angela in the kitchen, eating grapes. I sat with her and had a few grapes, too.

"I was waiting for you," she said.

I laughed. "Before I was the one waiting up for you, worried about you. That's a change."

"I'm not worried. I know you're okay with your Marine. I waited because I want to find out if, you know…"

"No, I don't know." But I did know.

She leaned closer to me, giggled and whispered, "Did he kiss you tonight?"

"That's none of your business."

She frowned. "That means no."

"It's too early. I need to know him better."

"My God, how much better do you need to know him? I practically know him well enough to kiss him myself."

"Don't even think about it."

"You should start thinking about it. You're not getting any younger, Luisa."

"We're taking it slowly," I said. "Besides, he's not an Italian. Americans aren't like that. It'll happen when it happens."

Angela rolled her eyes. "I hope by then you won't be too old to kiss, or even too old to..."

"Angela!"

She giggled.

My father came down the hall and poked his head into the kitchen. "What's all the noise?"

"Nothing, Papa. Go back to bed," Angela said.

My father looked straight at me. "You went out with that Marine again tonight?" His expression was hard, a strange anger underneath. I didn't understand why.

"He's a good man," I said.

"He's American."

Angela said, "That's not his fault."

"Twenty million Italian men and you pick an American."

Before I could answer, Angela said, "Papa, you don't have anything to worry about." She got up and walked to the doorway where he was standing. "They haven't even kissed yet," she said. "That's the problem with Americans." Angela kissed him on the cheek and headed up the hallway to her bedroom. "...'Night."

My father stood in the doorway, staring at me. I felt like I had to say something.

"He's a good man, Papa."

"You tell him you can't see him anymore."

"What? I'm not going to do that."

"You think you're going to marry him?"

"We're just friends," I said. "Nothing is happening."

"He's not for you, Luisa."

"I'm going to follow my heart, see what happens."

He came closer to the table and glared down at me. "I'll tell you what happens. You know he's a Marine, and when the time comes, they tell him he's done here, he's going to leave you. And then what are you going to do?"

"He's a nice guy."

He dismissed that thought with the flick of his hand. "That doesn't matter. The Marines tell him to go, he goes. And you, you follow your heart, you'll have a broken heart."

"I'm careful."

"Don't you understand?" He blew out a breath of exasperation. Struggling to control himself, he sat down next to me and said, "Listen to me. I only want what's best for you, and he's not what's best for you. I'm older than you. I know more, Luisa. You listen to me. I'm right."

I took his hand and said, "Papa, I'm not a little girl. I know what I'm doing."

He looked at me one more time, shook his head then went back to bed.

· · · · ·

A few weeks later, as we were driving back from a date in Naples, Brandon glanced at me in the darkness of the car and said, "I have something to tell you, Luisa."

His expression was so serious, I was afraid of what he was going to say. My father's words surfaced in my head. Brandon was leaving.

"What is it?" I asked. All this time with Brandon, practicing my English and studying the dictionary, I had learned a lot and we were able to communicate much better. I couldn't believe I had learned English this well, only to be told that he was leaving me.

He hesitated and then pulled the car over to the side of the road. When he turned off the engine, I found us in uncomfortable silence. A single car sped past. Then silence returned. Darkness surrounded us. I feared what was about to come.

He reached over and took my hands. "I want you to know that I love you," he said. "And the reason I didn't tell you this before, what I'm about to tell you, is because I didn't want to take the chance that you wouldn't see me again."

"Tell me what?" I asked.

"The minute I saw you and our eyes met, I knew you were for me."

I didn't understand. This isn't what you say when you are about to leave someone.

"What's wrong, Brandon?"

He hesitated again.

"Brandon," I started to say.

Then he blurted it out. "I'm not twenty-three years old, like I told you, and it's bothering me that I told you that, but I didn't want you to decide not to go out with me before you even got to know me."

I knew he was mature, but exactly how old was he. He had a young face. He couldn't be *that* much older than me. "How old are you?" I asked.

He hesitated, took a breath and said, "I am turning twenty."

I waited for the rest—twenty-what?—but he stopped. It took me a moment to understand what he was saying. He was four years younger than I was. I looked at him in shock. What had I done? How could I be with a man so much younger than I was? Husbands had to be older. My mother told me. My father told...Oh, no, my father was going to kill me. And kill Brandon.

"What I going to tell papa?" I said.

"Luisa, it's not a big deal. It's not such a big difference in age. And a lot of times the man is a little younger. There's nothing wrong with that."

"For you, no, because you are not Italian."

"No, that's because it's a fact."

"How you can lie to me, Brandon? I no understand."

"I'm sorry."

"You lie to me."

"It was wrong to lie, but I did it because I love you and I was afraid I'd lose you."

"Still you lie. How you can do this?"

"It was wrong, I know, but I'm sorry."

"Twenty," I said. "My God, you so young."

"Luisa, age doesn't matter. What I feel for you, that's all that matters."

"No, the age, it matters." He was too young for me. A husband couldn't be younger than his wife.

"Do you love me, Luisa?"

I didn't answer. I couldn't get it out of my head that he was so young, Angela's age, just a boy.

"Luisa," he said, squeezing my hands. "Look at me. Do you love me?"

I stared into his eyes and told him what was in my heart. "Yes, I love you."

"And I love you and that's all that matters."

"What I'm going to tell my father?"

"I'll tell your father."

"No," I said. That would never work. My father didn't need to know that right now. I would figure out that part. But something else bothered me. What else had Brandon lied about? I did not want to tie my life to someone who did not tell me the truth. I'd already had that, with Nino. Having broken that off, I was not going to repeat the same mistake.

"What more lies did you told me?" I asked.

"Nothing, honest."

"Tell me now, Brandon. I don't want no more surprise, like this."

"I swear, there's nothing else. And there never will be."

"I not going to with you, you lie to me," I said. "Is one thing I can no have."

"I swear to God that I'll never lie to you again. I swear it. I swear to God, to the Marine Corp, on my mother. I'll never lie to you again, Luisa. You mean everything to me. All I want is to be with you because I love you."

I stared into his eyes, and my heart told me to believe him.

CHAPTER 5

When I finally brought Brandon home to meet my father, I was not surprised that my father didn't like him. He was not rude to him, just cold. Afterward, my father again told me to forget about him, that he was going to leave me. That was the nature of American Marines.

"You think he's going to stay and make his life here? They all go home. This one is no different. And how will that leave you?"

I told my father not to worry, that I knew what I was doing. I didn't ask him, but I wondered if he cautioned me not so much out of concern for my having a broken heart, but more because he feared that more and more of my time would go toward Brandon and my own happiness, and less toward him and his happiness. He had already lost my mom. To him, Brandon meant another loss.

Brandon and I continued to see each other. After several weeks he invited me to go with him to Rome for a weekend.

"You told me that your mother used to take you to the Vatican every year," he said. "You haven't been there since she passed away so I'm going to take you this year myself. It's been long enough."

"You do that for me?" I asked.

Going there had always meant so much. My mother had had a strong faith and she had wanted to instill it in us as well. The yearly trips to the Vatican to see the Pope and receive his blessing, to feel the presence of the Holy Spirit, to refill the soul had always been special. When she had died, that ended, and I more than my brothers and sister truly missed it.

"You have to say yes," Brandon said.

· · · · ·

My father was upset when I told him I was going with Brandon to Rome, but I wasn't surprised. He saw that we were becoming increasingly serious and I saw that it worried him. But I had to live my life, just as my father had lived and still was living his. I didn't want to hurt him, and I reminded myself that any hurt he felt was imaginary. I wasn't supposed to take the place of my mother for him. And he wasn't losing his daughter. His daughter was growing up and finding her own path, the way everyone is supposed to.

We took the train to Rome on Saturday morning, left our bags at the hotel he'd found just a few blocks from Vatican City, and then went straight to St. Peter's Square. Tourists wandered about snapping photos and reading guidebooks aloud in more languages than I could identify. We passed a group of women who looked Eastern European, dressed in black and praying the rosary. As I stood in the shadow of the Basilica, my head filled with memories of my mother. I felt both happy and sad at the same time. I wiped the tear that snuck from my eye. I didn't want to cry.

Brandon put his arm around me, a comforting hug that instantly made me feel safe.

"It's okay," he said. "Your mom's probably watching and is happy that you're here."

"I know she is." I could feel her presence. I'd always had a strange awareness of things like that, a sense of things unseen, premonitions. It was not something I ever talked about. But it did guide me at times in my life.

This was one of those times that I felt this awareness, and it felt right, being here, being with Brandon.

We went into the Sistine Chapel, and I prayed for my mom and for the rest of my family. Brandon, who wasn't even Catholic, knelt down beside me and seemed to be praying. Afterwards we waited in line to see *La Pieta*, Michelangelo's marble statue of the Virgin Mary holding Jesus after he'd died. It was stunning to look at, even with people crowded all around us.

"Michelangelo had our age when he did this," I told Brandon.

He stared at it a long time and finally said, "Impressive. Michelangelo really left his mark on the world."

"Is one of the most great artist."

"I want to be like him," Brandon said.

"You an artist?"

"There's different ways to make your mark. I'm going to make mine, you'll see."

Looking at him and how he continued to stare at this masterpiece in front of us, seeing the conviction in his eyes, I definitely believed him.

• • • • •

Later that evening, when we arrived at a restaurant near the hotel, I thought we were just stopping to eat there because it had looked nice. But they had been expecting Brandon. They had a table waiting for us outside.

"You arranged this?" I asked.

"Of course. I wouldn't take you all the way to Rome without making sure it was special."

"Wow, I can no believe it."

Brandon held my chair for me. The night was warm and smelled sweet. Brandon waved his hand to someone in the piazza. A man selling roses hustled over. Without even asking the price, Brandon bought a bouquet for me and paid the man. As the waiter poured wine for both of us, a violin player approached, playing *"Io Te Vurria Vasà,"* the most romantic Napolitano song ever written.

I couldn't have been more impressed and moved. How could an American man be so romantic, more than any Italian I'd ever dated? I smiled to keep from crying.

When that song ended, the man immediately began playing a song I didn't recognize right away. Then, after a few notes, I realized what it was. Bryan Adams' "I Do It for You," the song we danced to that first night at the Marine dance. Brandon stood up and held out his hand for me to dance with him. I melted.

• • • • •

By the time we went back to the hotel, I felt like a princess. My knight in shining armor had spoiled me and protected me and made me feel special in a way I had never felt before.

He left the light off in the room. Through the window was the glow from St. Peter's dome, a dim light that illuminated the desire in Brandon's eyes. He slowly reached up and touched my shoulder. The feel of his skin against me made me shiver with a longing for more of his touch. His other hand glided up my other arm then held that shoulder.

I could feel how strong he was when without much effort he moved my body against his. I could feel his eagerness pressing against me. I peered up into his eyes.

"I want to make you feel pleasure in every possible way," he said. As he spoke, his lips moved slowly toward mine, and he kissed me. It lasted until I couldn't breathe any longer. When we parted, I barely had the air to speak.

"Make me feel," I whispered.

And he did. We didn't sleep at all that night. We made love over and over. Brandon kept going until I was exhausted, but I still didn't want to stop. I moaned for more. And that's what he gave me. I felt a rapture with him that I had never felt before. I'd only been with one other man, and that had been nothing like this. I knew then that this was love. What I had had with Nino hadn't even been close.

After we went back to Naples, it was as if we had unleashed something that could not be contained again. Our love, both physical and emotional. We made love again in my father's apartment when everyone else had gone out for a short while. We did it over and over, not wanting to stop, but fearing that my father or one of my siblings was going to come in and catch us.

Brandon became so much a part of my life that I had to see him every day, touch him, feel his body close to mine. One time, when I hadn't seen him for two days, I missed him terribly and began to wonder if something was wrong. I called him several times, but he didn't answer. When night came, I drove to the base. I needed to see him.

The atmosphere outside the gate was strangely quiet. At first the Marines standing guard told me I had to go, but I knew them. They were friends of Brandon that I'd met on several of our dates, and when they recognized me, they agreed to call Brandon and let him know I was outside.

It wasn't long before he arrived and came outside the gate. His Marine friends stayed on the other side, trying to give us some privacy, but they all looked nervous. Brandon did, too. He was carrying a rifle and wearing his camouflage uniform. He had always been happy to see me, no matter where were. But tonight for the first time he seemed not to want me there.

"Why you haven't called me, Brandon?" I asked.

"You have to go, Luisa."

"Why aren't you calling me?"

"I can't talk now. You need to go. The base is under alert."

"What does that mean?"

"It means you can't be here. I'm going to get into trouble."

"Brandon." I needed him. I reached up to touch him and he quickly took a step back.

"Don't," he said. He lowered his voice. "Luisa, there are guns pointed at you right now. It isn't safe. Please go home. I'll call you when this is all over."

I didn't know if it was his harshness with me, or fear for his safety, or just that I needed him and couldn't have him, but I started to cry and needed him to hold me. But he didn't.

"I love you," he whispered, and I could see that it was taking all his strength for him not to hug and comfort me. "You don't understand. It will be okay. I promise. Just go home. I'll call you when I can."

Somehow I made it back to my car and drove home. I cried much of the night. Days passed before I was finally able to talk to him on the phone. He explained that a woman had showed up at the base earlier, and she'd had explosives strapped to her body. The Marines didn't know if I was another terrorist, there to blow them up. Brandon told me that someone complained to his commander, and questioned him about me, accusing me of being a suicide bomber or a prostitute.

I wanted to cry when I heard that, but I was heartened when Brandon told me that he insisted to the commander, "No, sir. She is my girlfriend."

· · · · ·

A few months later, Brandon was again stuck on the base and I had to go without seeing him. One day, after fighting with my father and with Rodolfo, and after working all day and no one appreciating me, I really needed my boyfriend, so I called Brandon and told him how important it was that I see him.

He told me to wait two hours then drive to the base and park my Fiat alongside the wall in a dark area out of view from the gate. He said not to get out of the car, just park and wait. I did as told, feeling a tingle of excitement that we were breaking the rules for love. I waited for a few minutes, and then out of the shadows came a tall figure in camouflage. At first I couldn't tell who it was and I started to think of what I was going to say, but then I saw Brandon's face. He slid into the car beside me and kissed me hard.

"I'm crazy about you," he said when our lips parted. "I know you're going to get me into trouble."

"I miss you."

"I miss you too, but you have to understand, I'm a Marine and Marines can't always leave the base when they want. We have to follow orders. I need you to understand, Luisa."

"I understand, but..."

"No buts," he said. "This is the last time this can happen. Okay?"

I nodded. "I'm sorry," I said.

"You don't have to be sorry, just understand."

He kissed me and said, "Now you go home. I'll call you when..."

Before he could finish, I kissed him, smothering his words. I couldn't control my feelings. This kiss was much longer and more passionate, and before I knew what was happening, we were peeling off each other's clothes. We made love, bent into the front seat of the car, in the darkness along the wall of the base.

When we had finished, I was surprised at myself that I could be so free and wild.

Someone saw us making love in the car that night and reported Brandon. His punishment was thirty days confinement to his room. There was also a threat that they would take his corporal's rank away from him and make him a private again.

"I'm so sorry, is all my fault," I told him on the phone. "Is not fair that you punished."

He wasn't even supposed to have phone privileges, but a buddy of his bent the rules so he could call me.

"No, it's my fault," he said. "I wanted to see you. It's my responsibility."

"I don't know what I'm going to do, not to see you for thirty days. My God."

"Listen, my love, I'll call you in a few days. I have a plan."

"What do you mean?"

"I'll let you know in a few days."

. . . . .

He did call three days later.

"My love," he said, "Can you be at the west gate at six pm? Just park your car and wait."

It was summer and the days were long. It was still light out when I arrived. I parked as instructed and waited. I decided that if I got caught, I wasn't going to mention Brandon so he wouldn't get into further trouble.

A few minutes later a Marine approached the car. He came up to my opened window.

"Are you Lance Corporal Cloutier's girlfriend?"

"No," I said. I didn't understand Brandon's plan, how he was going to get outside, but something had gone wrong.

"No?" the Marine said.

"No, I just waiting for a friend."

The Marine leaned over, closer to the window and spoke in a low voice. "Brandon sent me to get you and bring you to him, if you're Luisa."

Until Forever

Bring me to him? How is that possible? "Yes, I'm Luisa. How can..."

He held up his hand to stop my question. "Just do what I say please, Ma'am."

He opened the door and gestured for me to get out. I did. I had done my best to look good for Brandon, with make-up, a tight dress that complimented my curves, a tailored jacket. My high heels clattered on the pavement as I walked.

"Just stay by my side," the Marine said as we headed toward the gate, "and don't say a word. Have your ID ready."

I did as he said. We walked to the gate. He showed his Marine ID the way Brandon always did when he took me onto the base to go to the club or the restaurant. I showed the guard my ID. I didn't know if I was supposed to smile or not, so I didn't. I barely looked at the man checking documents. The Marine Brandon sent kept walking. I didn't wait for the guard to gesture me in. I just stayed beside Brandon's friend.

The base was fairly busy that evening. Marines hurrying to get from one building to the next. A few were tossing an American football on a grassy area. Humvees roared by. We headed toward the big building that I had been inside many times before. I felt giddy with anticipation. We were obviously doing something wrong, but I was doing it in order to see the man I loved and that made it exciting.

Without even looking at me, Brandon's friend said out of the corner of his mouth, quietly, so no one else could hear, "When I say run, you run. Follow me."

I nodded.

When we reached the building, instead of going in through the main entrance, he led me to another doorway with stairs going down. He checked to make sure no one was looking and then opened the door and gestured for me to go inside.

As soon as I did, he rushed in behind me, pulled the door shut and yelled, "Run!"

He took off. The hallway snaked through the basement. It was empty except for us. I followed the Marine around a couple sharp turns. He pulled open a door and practically pushed me through. He bounded up the stairs on the other side. In my high heels, I struggled to follow, clutching the railing to keep from falling.

We ran up four or five flights—I lost count how many—before he finally stopped at a door on the landing. He held up his hand for me to stop and wait. Then he inched open the door and peeked out. Another Marine was standing on the other side of the door. I wasn't sure if we had gotten caught.

"Clear?" the one helping me asked this other Marine.

"Clear."

The first Marine turned to me. "Good luck, Ma'am."

I didn't understand what was happening.

The new Marine looked down at me and said, "Evening, Ma'am. Are you ready to run some more?"

My feet hurt and I was perspiring under my dress and jacket, but I had never been more ready to run than I was at that moment. I nodded.

"Let's go then."

· · · · ·

When we reached Brandon's room, I could not believe what had just happened. I felt like I was in a movie. I was giddy with excitement, and not only because of what I'd done to get here, but more so because I was finally going to see Brandon. The door opened and there he was.

He took me into his arms and nothing else existed or mattered. I was with him. I would have done anything to get here, to be with him. We started kissing and he began to take off my dress.

"What if someone comes in?" I whispered.

"Don't worry about that, my love. My boys are watching outside. You're safe with me here."

CHAPTER 6

My mother had died on the 11th of November. Exactly three years after to the day was when Brandon wanted me to take me to the Marine Corps birthday celebration. It was the biggest event on the base, the biggest celebration for any Marine.

I couldn't believe how understanding Brandon was when I told him I couldn't possibly celebrate on the same day as my mother's death. He told me he didn't want me to do anything that would make me sad. "Don't even think about it anymore," he told me.

But I did think about it. He said he had to go, all the Marines did. I kept thinking about him being there alone, was I being fair to him? How long was I supposed to give up that terrible day? I would mourn my mother's death forever. But at some point I would need to continue with my life. My father seemed to have. He had a girlfriend. He rarely talked about my mother. On the anniversary of her death he was scheduled to work. My brothers and sister, too, were not reserving that day for sadness. For me, though, it seemed wrong to be laughing and dancing and drinking and having a party on the day my mother had been ripped away.

Mom's sister Gianna must have had that date on her mind, too, because she came to the apartment a few days before the Marines' party to see how everyone was doing. I was the only one home, doing my usual chores. We sat down at the kitchen and I made a pot of espresso.

"You're really the one I wanted to see," Aunt Gianna said.

"Me? Why?"

"Sometimes I think you're the one holding the family together. Your father has his qualities, sure, but being the family glue isn't one of them. And the other kids, they look to you the way they used to look to Lina. It must be hard on you."

I had never complained to her or to anyone else. I did what I promised my mother I'd do. "Everyone has obligations," I said. "It isn't easy for any of us."

"Of course not." But I could see by her expression that she didn't believe that. She changed the subject. "Tell me about that boyfriend of yours." Gianna hadn't met him yet. "When am I going to see him?" she asked.

I shrugged, thinking again about the party.

"What's the matter?" Gianna asked.

I took a breath and explained it all.

As soon as I was done, she took me by the hand and said, "Luisa, listen to me. You're going to that party."

"I can't. Mamma would not appreciate it."

She gawked at me in disbelief. "You think your mamma would want you to be a nun, to lose a good man that you love, to give up your dreams. Are you crazy?"

"No, but..."

"No, no, no." Zia Gianna wasn't going to listen. "No buts. You're going. Now, what are you going to wear?"

"I don't have anything to wear anyway and the party's only a couple days away."

She practically pulled me out of the chair. "Let's go," she said.

"What? Go where?"

"I have a beautiful sequined jacket you can borrow. We're going to pick out a dress, get you some new shoes, go to the hairdresser. You're going to be beautiful. You're already beautiful, you're going to be *more* beautiful."

• • • • •

I wore a black chiffon dress that I had bought for a friend's wedding over the summer. Enzo did my hair and makeup as if I were going to a red carpet event in Milan. With Zia Gianna's sequined jacket and the new black suede high heels with crystals on them that I had bought, I felt like a princess on the way to the ball.

Brandon arrived to pick me up in a uniform I hadn't seen before, white dress pants, white shoes, a deep blue jacket and a white hat. His hair, which was usually short, was cut even tighter. He had just shaved and he smelled of cologne. My prince.

His lips formed into a huge smile as he stared at me. "You look so beautiful," he said.

I felt myself blush. His compliments always made me feel self-conscious. In Italy men are always complimenting women, didn't matter if they knew you or not, if they or you were married or not. That didn't affect me at all. I was used to it. But when it came from someone whose words meant something to me, then it was very different. From Brandon it meant something.

"Don't be shy," he said, as he took me by the hand. "You look too good to be shy."

But I was so nervous I was shaking as he took me to his car.

"What's the matter, my love?" he asked.

"I'm worried."

"There's nothing to worry about."

"There is lot to be worry. All those fancy people there. Your commander. The officers. Everyone. This is a important thing. My English is not so good. I'm worried I'm going to…"

"What? First of all, your English is great. You speak better English than half the guys in the platoon. There a couple privates from Alabama, sound like their speaking another language altogether. And Sergeant Connelly, he mumbles so much no one understands him most of the time. Believe me, you won't have any problem at all with language."

I laughed, but I knew my English wasn't as good as most of the people there, nowhere near as good as the American girlfriends and wives. They were going to look at me as inferior. Honestly, I didn't care what they thought of me. They weren't my friends. I didn't have to spend time with them beyond tonight. But Brandon saw them all the time, and I didn't want them to think less of him because he was with me.

He must have seen the uneasiness in my face, even though I was trying to smile, because he held me tightly and said, "You're with me, Luisa. You're going to be fine. I'll make sure of that."

He was the first and only man that, when he said those words, I truly knew he would.

                                       ○   ○   ○   ○   ○

When we arrived at the celebration, it was like something out of a movie. All the Marines in their dress uniforms. Beautiful women in their best dresses. A live band. The best food. Brandon treated me like I was special, not little Luisa La Rotonda from Giugliano, Italy, but instead like someone who belonged at fancy events like this, by his side. He held my chair and made sure I had something to drink, made sure they bought me everything I wanted to eat, focused his attention completely on me.

Three other couples sat at the same table with us. I was the only Italian. I felt the other women looking at me strangely. No none said anything bad to me, but something about the way they looked at me, the way they avoided talking to me, made it clear that they saw me differently. Maybe as less than they were. Or maybe as a threat. I couldn't tell. But there was definitely a barrier between us.

It became most clear when a Marine came over and said he needed all of the men because they Marines were going to take group picture together. Brandon excused himself and left with the others, telling me that it would be okay, it would only be a second, he'd be right back.

I took a sip of wine to fortify myself to be alone and smiled at the women surrounding me.

Two of them smiled back. One said something to the woman beside her too soft and rapid for me to figure out the English. The one she spoke to giggled. I wondered if they were talking about me.

"So, Lisa," the third woman said. "We don't know much about you. What do you do?"

"Is Luisa," I said.

"Oh. Sorry."

"After my mother she die, I take care the house."

"Oh." She nodded and avoided looking at me. "That's...nice."

"Do you go to school or something, Lisa?" the one who had giggled asked.

I shook my head no.

"That's okay." Her tone was condescending, something we weren't used to in Italy. Italians will talk about you or criticize you if they don't like you, but they do it directly, and they'll have a reason for it. "Maybe some day, right?" she said.

The way they were talking to me, looking at me, I felt so uncomfortable I wanted to leave. I felt tears pooling behind my eyes and my throat began to swell, ready to cry, but I didn't want them to see this. And I didn't want to let Brandon down. I fought to hold it in. I didn't speak, knowing that if I opened my mouth I'd either tell them what I thought of them or I'd start crying.

The one who had whispered to the other woman earlier now looked at me and said, "We were wondering who the woman was that took Brandon off the market. He had a lot of girls after him, you know."

"I know," I said, though I really hadn't known, nor did I care. I just wanted them to see me being strong and confident.

"Well," the giggler said, her eyes sweeping over me as through she were looking at item in the store she was about to reject. "You're not what I imagined, Lisa."

"My name is Luisa," I said, glaring at the three of them. I was not going to let myself cry. Not in front of them. "You may no remember my name," I said, blurting out the only thing I could think to say. "But I guarantee you, you men do."

Three mouths fell open. Three pairs of eyes stared at me. Not a word came out of any of them. I had no interest in their husbands or boyfriends or whatever they were, but I just wanted to get back at them for being so rude. And it worked.

Just then Brandon hurried over. "Luisa, come with me," he said. "I want to get a picture with you."

"Are you sure?" I asked.

"Yes, I'm very sure. You're so beautiful. I want to remember forever how beautiful you look tonight."

The three women stared in silence. I could tell that Brandon's praise of me devastated them. They were so jealous, they hated me. I loved it.

And I realized how much I loved Brandon. He didn't care what anyone else thought about me, how anyone else saw me, whether anyone else was even in the room with me and him. He saw me for who I was and he loved who I was. I had so much fear of relationships, of men leaving, of letting someone in only to lose them, of loving someone and being loved back less. But my heart was telling me that Brandon was the man. I needed to follow my heart.

CHAPTER 7

In April, on my twenty-fourth birthday, Brandon came over with roses and a Caravel Ice Cream cake. We have some of the best pastries in Italy. The cakes that local bakeries make for birthdays are incredible, but in twenty-four years I had never had a cake made out of ice cream. It was the coolest thing.

He also gave me a gold Gucci watch that was so elegant and beautiful I couldn't believe it was really for me. I'd never had anything like it before in my life. He put it on me and told me that I was more valuable and special than even the finest jewelry. It was my best birthday ever.

"You are the most important person in my life," I told him when we were alone. "I love you with all my heart."

"And I love you, Luisa."

Three weeks later, Brandon came over to the apartment to see me. I thought it was just a regular visit, but before I knew what was happening, he got down on one knee. It suddenly struck me what he was doing.

I gasped. "Oh, my God."

He looked up at me and smiled. His eyes saw straight into my heart.

"I don't have a ring yet," he said.

His words touched me, but at the same time they filled me with such fear, I thought I was going to fall apart. I couldn't speak. I could barely breathe.

"But I promise you I'm going to get you the best ring," he said. "I just can't wait for that. I need to do this."

"Oh, Brandon," I said, the only words I was able to get out.

"You're the best thing to ever happen to me, Luisa. Ever since I met you, I've been the happiest man on earth. I don't want to spend a day without you. I love you so much. I want you to marry me."

His eyes were so sincere, his words so wonderful to hear. It was like a scene from an American movie. I couldn't believe it was really happening to me.

"Please stand up," I said. "I no want you on your knees for me."

But he remained there. He grasped my hands and again said, "Luisa, marry me."

I knew what I had to say. It wasn't easy.

"Brandon, I love you. But I can no marry you."

"What do you mean you *can't*? Are you saying you don't want to?"

"Is no it." All my adult life, all I wanted was to marry a man who would love me unconditionally, give me security and not cheat on me. If anyone was that man, it was Brandon.

"Don't you understand," I said. "I can no leave my family? They need me."

"I need you."

I smiled. "No you don't."

"Yes I do. Not to cook dinner and clean and wash my clothes, no. I need you more deeply than that. I love you and I want to spend the rest of my life with you."

"But I..."

He held up his hand and stopped me. "Luisa, they're shipping me back to California."

His words were like blows to my stomach. I struggled to breathe. I couldn't believe it. My father's warning was coming true. He was going to leave.

"Come with me," he said.

"I can't."

"You keep saying that."

"Because is true. My family needs me to take care of them."

"No they don't. You have to make your own life, Luisa. They all are. You can't live the rest of your life for them. You've done it long enough."

In my head I reasoned that he was probably right, but in my heart it felt selfish, like a betrayal to my mother, like I was abandoning the family.

"Come at least to see what it's like there," he said. "Meet my family. Then you decide."

"I don't know..."

I had always wanted to leave Naples, leave Italy. There was a big world out there and I was desperate to experience it. But I had promised my mother. Besides, it was one thing to dream of leaving. Another thing to actually pick up and go.

"Don't say no yet. Please. Promise me you'll think about it. Okay? Really think about it."

"I think about it. Maybe if I can save some money for a ticket..."

"Is that it? I'm paying for the ticket," he said, as if it should have been obvious. "I'll take care of everything. Is that what's bothering you?"

"You can no understand," I said. "Is more than that. Let me think about it, okay?"

. . . . .

When I told my father, his first reaction was to get angry. He yelled that I was crazy. He said he'd told me that Brandon would leave. He scolded me for even thinking about leaving the family.

"Who's going to take care of your brothers and sister?" I was sure he meant who was going to take care of him.

Later, calmly, sadly, he asked me not to go.

"It's only for three months, Papa," I said. That was all the visa would allow me to stay in American. "I have to come back."

My father shook his head. He didn't believe me.

"It's the truth, Papa."

"You're going to do what you want to do," he said. "But you have a family here, Luisa. This is where you come from. This is where you belong. With your family. Not in America or anywhere else. Think about your sister and your brothers."

"I do, Papa. You know I do. But then tell me something. Who thinks about me?"

"Your family is forever. An American Marine is here one day. The next day, poof. I think about you. I don't want you to be hurt. I don't want you to make a mistake."

He left me with those words, with his wishes very clear. But what was not clear was which thing was the mistake, going to American or staying here.

My little sister Angela came to my room that night. She'd heard what my father had said. She walked over to my bed, where I was lying, staring at the ceiling, praying and struggling with what to do. She lay beside me and hugged me. My first thought was that she, too, was telling me not to leave.

"Luisa," she said. "You have to go. Don't listen to Papa about this. I know you're afraid. But if you don't go—or at least to see what it's all about—you're going to regret it for the rest of your life."

PART TWO

CHAPTER 8

SUMMER 1993
Boston, Massachusetts

When I arrived at the airport in Boston with a three month visa to stay in the US, I was worried about what would happen when I stepped out into the terminal. I went through customs and immigration, so nervous they looked at me suspiciously, but eventually they stamped my passport and passed me through.

Pulling my suitcase behind me, I followed the other passengers through the automatic doors and into the waiting area of the international terminal. A low railing kept the people waiting twenty feet away. Behind that railing hundreds of people formed a wall directly in front of me. On either side, also held at bay by restraining railings, were more people. Narrow spaces were left open to the right and to the left, allowing passengers to exit. The scene was confusing and overwhelming. I wasn't sure which direction to go until I heard Brandon's voice.

"Luisa!"

I looked to the right. Brandon came running toward me, smiling. He'd had to return earlier and we hadn't gone this long without seeing each other in more than a year. Before I could start toward him, he covered the ground between us, grabbed me and lifted me off the ground as if I weighed nothing. I started to worry that the other people in the terminal would think we were crazy, but then I decided that didn't matter. All that mattered was that we were together again. We kissed with desperation. The scent of his cologne, the passion in his lips and strength of his arms around me dominated my senses.

When he finally put me down, he grabbed my suitcase with one hand, grasped my hand with the other and said, "Come on. I want you to meet my brother and his fiancée."

His brother Shane didn't look much like him, but he welcomed me with a friendly handshake. People had told me that Americans don't hug a lot unless they know you very well. I assumed I would get used to it, but it felt strange. His fiancée Dina smiled and shook my hand too. I really couldn't tell if they liked me or not. Brandon liked me. That much I could tell. He put his arm around me and we all walked to Shane's car parked outside.

* * * * *

Brandon and I sat together in the back seat on the drive to his grandmother's house. Still so happy to be together again, we hugged and kissed most of the time. Brandon was staying with his grandmother in Hudson, forty-five minutes away from Boston. To get there Shane took a highway that had us cutting right through the center of the city. Tall buildings were everywhere. Thousands of cars sped alongside us. More cars were crowded on the city streets below us.

I kept thinking, *My God, I'm in a country, a different world.* I was thrilled to be out of Naples, thrilled to be here, but I was still nervous. I looked over at Brandon. Sometimes we had this way of communicating that did not involve words. We spoke with our eyes. This was one of those times. He seemed to understand exactly what I was feeling. He pulled me a little closer and held me protectively the whole way.

When we arrived in Hudson and left the highway, Brandon pointed out the significant things that we passed on our way to his grandmother's house. "There," he said. "That's where I went to high school." A little later. "Over there's where I used to go sledding when it snowed. Do you like snow?"

"We don't have snow in Napoli."

"It's great, you'll love it."

"It snows in the summer?" I asked. "My visa is no more after October."

He just waved that off and said, "We'll see about that."

I knew that three months was the longest they would let me stay. But I didn't want to think about that right now. I wanted to enjoy the present with Brandon.

"And over there," he said, pointing again.

I was glad that we were going back to happy things again.

"Over there is where Uncle Dennis is buried."

. . . . .

I never could have expected such a warm welcome from his family when we reached his grandmother's house. I found out later that his grandmother practically raised him for many years. She hugged me enough to almost be an Italian. Brandon's grandfather and uncle seemed to like me as well. Even Brandon's mother treated me like someone they had been waiting for forever. So much different from the way my father was when he met Brandon.

They kept saying how beautiful I was. No one seemed to mind that my English wasn't very good. Everybody wanted to meet me and they all sat around me in the living room, asking all kinds of questions, many of which I didn't understand. I answered a lot with smiles. That seemed to be okay. Brandon sat close to me. I felt he was protecting me.

Amid all the happiness and hospitality, I noticed Shane and Dina looking at me strangely a few times. Dina especially. She didn't talk much, just watched. Her stare made me a bit uneasy.

At one point, when I excused myself to use the bathroom, I saw her in the kitchen on my way back. She was putting some cookies on a plate. I stopped and asked her if I could help.

"I'm good."

I wasn't sure what that meant, so I looked around for something I could do. "You live far?" I asked.

"Across the street," she said.

"Oh, wow. Is great. Then we see each other a lot," I said.

Dina shook her head. "Probably not. Between work and all the things I have to do, I'm not around so much."

"Oh. Okay. Well, maybe the evening."

"I didn't think you were going to stay around here *that* long, are you? I mean, aren't you going to California pretty soon?"

"I go where Brandon say." I was letting him plan this visit.

"Uh huh."

She took the tray of cookies and went back into the living room. I decided she didn't like me very much. But I was sure I didn't do anything wrong. I followed and tried not to let her get me down.

For dinner Brandon took me out to what he said was an Italian Restaurant. The menu had some Italian foods listed on it, but the cooks must have been from Bosnia. They definitely weren't Italian. The pasta was overcooked, the tomato sauce bitter. The *caprese* salad had been made with refrigerated tomatoes that had lost their taste and with shredded mozzarella that belonged in a pizza, not in a *caprese*. I could have eaten a package that tasted the same. Not packaged *caprese*, but the package itself.

I honestly didn't mind, though. It was so nice that he would try to make me feel comfortable by taking me to what he thought was an Italian restaurant. Brandon wouldn't let me pay for anything.

I asked him about Dina. "I don't know why she don't like me."

"Forget about her," he said. "She's jealous."

"Jealous?"

"You're getting all the attention, Luisa. She's used to being the young woman around. It doesn't help that you're so beautiful."

I felt my face blush. "I'm not so beautiful."

"You're right. Beautiful doesn't begin to describe you. You're beyond beautiful. You're...*bellissima!*"

"You always so good to me," I said.

He took hold of my hands. "You're the woman of my dreams."

"You are too," I said.

He smiled. "I always wanted to be the woman of your dreams."

· · · · ·

That night, we argued about who was going to sleep where. The rule in Brandon's grandparents' house was that you couldn't sleep together if you weren't married. Brandon wanted me to take the bedroom upstairs that belonged to Uncle Bobby, who wasn't there, and Brandon would sleep on the sofa in the living room. I insisted I sleep on the sofa. I didn't want to take his room away, and I felt uneasy sleeping upstairs with his grandparents.

In the end, I got the sofa. I really didn't mind sleeping on the sofa, but I just wished it wasn't so far away from Brandon's room. It would have been better if he were downstairs. Just having him nearby, I would have felt safer. I was a little nervous. It Italy, we often heard about how much crime there was in America. And even though this house seemed quiet and safe—in fact everything I had seen in Hudson seemed that way—I was in a new place that I didn't fully understand yet and that left me feeling nervous.

It was also a lot colder than I thought it would be, especially at night. Brandon saw how cold I was and gave me an extra blanket before he went upstairs. As I tucked myself under it, I wondered if maybe it did actually snow in Massachusetts during the summer.

Exhausted from the trip and from all the activity since I landed, I fell asleep quickly and slept soundly. That is, until the middle of the night. I awoke to the sensation of someone touching my chest. I was about to scream when I saw a cat sitting on top of me, staring at me. I stared back, thinking it was going to run away. It didn't move.

"*Buona sera*," I said.

The cat meowed.

"*Capisci Italiano?*"

The cat meowed again then started to purr. I reached over and petted it. It purred louder and came even closer. Maybe it did understand Italian.

It stayed on me all night. Eventually I drifted off to sleep again. Brandon was there when I woke up, holding a cup of coffee for me. The cat was still there.

"I can't believe she slept here with you," he said.

"Why not?"

"She never liked any girlfriend I brought home. She always tried to scratch them."

"Oh, so you brought a lot of girls home?" I said.

"I wouldn't say a lot. Twelve hundred or so."

I swung at him playfully. We both laughed.

"No, not many. But you're the first girl she liked. I guess that means you're the one for me."

"You let the cat decide?"

"I already decided a long time ago. I'm just waiting for you to come to the same decision."

· · · · ·

That day I met more of Brandon's family and saw more of the village he came from. There really wasn't much to see or do, but I was satisfied just to see where he came from.

For dinner he took me again to the Italian restaurant. I tried the *melanzana* but it was too dry and had some strange seasonings in it. It tasted like they used cheap oil too. Cheap oil upsets the stomach. I couldn't finish my plate.

"You don't like it?" Brandon said. "You can order something else."

"No, is okay. I'm just not so hungry."

"You hate it, don't you?"

"No. Is nice you want to take to Italian food. But is just not the same..."

"You hate it, don't you?" he said again.

I laughed. "I said, no. Is okay."

"I'll find a better place for tomorrow."

"No, you don't have to. I'm in a new place. The food isn't like Italy. Is like here. I have to adjust is all."

"I'm still going to find a better place."

"Why are you so kind to me?" I asked.

His concern for my happiness always surprised me. I was sure that one day it would suddenly stop. From my personal experiences, men were not this kind and unselfish. They didn't think of the woman first. Brandon was different. His first priority seemed to make me happy.

In many ways he was different from the men I'd known all of my life. I realized as I sat with him in that American restaurant with bad Italian food that he was probably the man I was meant to be with. He was everything I had always dreamed of, in every way. Superficially he was tall and muscular with blond hair and blue eyes. If I had drawn my dream man, he would have looked exactly like Brandon. And deep inside, he had such a generous, caring heart. He really wanted to make me happy. And he didn't lie and cheat on me and disappear when it was convenient. He also was not in Naples, and I had been desperate to leave there. I used to pray for someone like Brandon. God must have heard my prayers and sent me this American Marine.

I had endured so much suffering over the last few years. Finally something good had come to me. I was so glad I had agreed to come here to meet his family and see if I liked America.

. . . . .

The next day, Brandon's Uncle Bobby came to Brandon's grandparents' house. Brandon wasn't too happy to see him. I saw disgust in his eyes.

"What's wrong?" I asked Brandon.

Brandon sighed. "He drinks sometimes."

"He looks okay." He looked like a person who had been through a difficult life, with a rugged face and bent up body, but I didn't think he was drunk.

"For now," Brandon said. "But he's going to want his room back."

Brandon was right. Uncle Bobby was happy to see Brandon, slapping him on the back and repeating, "You look good, Brandon, the Marines did you good," and friendly toward me, but he did put his things into his bedroom. Shane came over and told us to come stay at his place.

"You have room?" Brandon asked. "It's okay with Dina?"

"Of course." As he, Brandon and I walked across the street with my suitcase and Brandon's duffle bag, Shane said, "And in my house, I don't have any rule about not sleeping in the same room if you're not married."

The first evening went okay. Shane was welcoming to us, trying to make us feel comfortable. Dina didn't say much to me, though. I didn't know what to do so she would get over any jealousy, if that's what she felt. I just tried to be nice to her.

After we all went to bed, the night became wonderful. I was so happy to sleep in the same room and same bed with Brandon. We made love that first night, as quietly as possible because we didn't want Shane and Dina to hear. But it was difficult not to make noise. Brandon knew exactly where and how to touch me, how to make me feel. He gave me orgasm after orgasm. I bit my lip to keep from shrieking with pleasure but some noise came out anyway. He moaned, too, as he came. We both laughed afterward, wondering if his Shane and Dina had heard and what they were thinking.

The next morning at breakfast, they didn't say much to us and almost never looked us in the face. I was sure they knew. Brandon told me not to worry. They went to work. Brandon borrowed his grandmother's car and drove me to Boston to see the sights there. We had a great time together. Everywhere we went, he made sure I had whatever I wanted and he never let me pay for a thing. I was his princess, and I loved it.

When we returned to Hudson in the evening, Shane's house was strangely quiet. We found him sitting alone in the living room with few lights on.

"Where's Dina?" Brandon asked.

"She went upstairs."

It wasn't *that* late, I thought.

"Did you guys eat dinner yet?" Brandon asked.

Shane shook his head. "She's kind of pissed at me."

"Why? What happened?"

"Ah, nothing." Shane glanced at the stairs and then whispered, "You know how she gets."

Brandon just nodded. He looked at me. I could see that he felt embarrassed having me in the middle of this situation.

"Maybe we should just go bed," he told Shane.

"Yeah, well, I've got talk to you about that, Brandon," Shane said.

"What's up?"

Shane looked at me then quickly turned away. He had a hard time looking at Brandon, too, as he said, "It's not a good idea for you guys to stay tonight."

Brandon stared at his brother. I saw something in his eyes that I had never seen before. I couldn't tell if it was anger or something else. He remained silent. Shane continued.

"I mean if it was up to me, I'd..."

"Forget it, man," Brandon said.

"No, but you know how it is," Shane said, gesturing toward the upstairs.

"Forget it." Brandon took my hand. "Come on, Luisa."

"I'm sorry, Brandon."

"I know."

"Just for tonight."

"Yeah."

Brandon took me outside into the night air. Insects and frogs made weird noises from the darkness behind the houses. I looked into Brandon's eyes and realized that what I had seen was humiliation and shame.

"Don't worry 'bout it," I told him.

"I'm sorry, Luisa. I'm so sorry. This isn't fair to you."

"Brandon, I don't care where I go, long as I'm with you."

. . . . .

In the driveway of Brandon's grandparents was a green Ford van. Brandon explained that this was where his grandparents sent Uncle Bobby when he showed up drunk, instead of letting him into the house.

He pulled open the door. Inside it smelled of mildew and sweat. An old mattress covered the floor. There was also an empty bottle of some kind of alcohol and a dirty tee-shirt. Brandon told me to wait while he picked up the trash and put the sheets his grandmother had given him onto the mattress. Having the doors open for a few minutes helped to air it out a bit. It was cold, but at least the stench was tolerable. Brandon kept apologizing. I really didn't mind. As long as I was in his arms, I was okay.

As night settled heavily over the van and the sound of frogs and bugs closed in around us, we again made passionate love and I again felt in my heart that I had found the man of my dreams. I did not want to ever let him go.

CHAPTER 9

When it was time for Brandon to go back to the base in California, I was ready to leave Hudson and see more of the United States. Brandon was stationed at Twenty-nine Palms, a Marine base in the middle of the desert, two and a half hours from Los Angeles. I could not stay on the base with him, but I had a friend, Maria, from Italy who had moved to Los Angeles.

Maria's boyfriend was an American Marine still stationed in Italy. She was alone and she offered to let me stay with her. It was perfect for me because I was still learning English and could converse with her in Italian, so I didn't feel completely away from everything I knew. I had company for when Brandon was on the base and I was with Maria. Plus she was looking for someone to help take care of her son, Corey, who had Cystic Fibrosis, so it worked out well for her too.

She didn't have an extra bedroom, but the laundry room was large enough to fit a mattress on the floor, so that became my room. I didn't mind. I didn't need a lot of room. I lived out of my suitcases and only used the room to sleep and to study my English-Italian dictionary.

Brandon borrowed a car and drove down the first weekend. He took me to see Hollywood and Venice Beach. I was amazed at everything. He also took me to have my first Mexican food, which was fun even though it didn't sit well with my stomach. He reserved a room at a hotel in Marina Del Ray, and it was so good to be with him again. We made love with no fear of any family coming in or any commanding officer finding out and implementing a punishment. It was magical.

Watching him drive away Sunday night was the hard part. It meant another week without him. I hated being apart from him, but I understood that he was doing the best he could. I had to make the best of it. Until he returned on the next weekend, I was on my own.

Days were spent with Corey, who I took care of when Maria went to work. This took up much of my time. But I loved it. He had such passion for life and was a joy to be around. Cystic Fibrosis was only one element of who he was. It was a chronic disease that he had. It was not him. Managing it, however, was not easy.

Maria told me that it was important to be disciplined with his schedule. He had to eat a lot of high protein, high fat foods, usually more than he wanted. And he had to eat often. His enzymes, which he swallowed with all of his meals, had to be taken like clockwork. So too for his medications, his breathing treatments and his chest therapy. All of these were essential in keeping his breathing as close to normal as possible.

Sometimes, when his lungs became congested and he struggled so much to breathe that his skin color became frighteningly pale, I would have so spend hours pounding on his back to break up the mucus membranes so that he could breathe.

California weather was beautiful, a sunny warmth that seemed to be eternal, each day the same. I took him for walks often. He couldn't go far, but he relished being outside and soaking up a few California rays. He also loved to play and he had a talent for drawing and art. We spent hours on the floor, Corey making pictures, each one he showed me with the pride of a Renaissance artist. Aside from drawing books and crayons, Maria bought him all kinds of toys, and unlike most kids who took their toys for granted, played with them only once and then discarded them, Corey never lost interest.

He found fascination in most of what he did, and that always impressed me. With all that he was going through, he seemed to try to take a bite out of life every day. Whenever I started to miss Brandon or miss my family back home in Naples, or lament the difficulties I had endured over the years, I would take one look at Corey and immediately get over myself.

I spent a lot of time studying my English-Italian dictionary. Being with Brandon, my English was getting better, but I wanted to be able to say everything, to tell him everything and to understand everything he said to me, so I spent hours each day looking in my dictionary, memorizing words. I also learned by watching TV with Corey. The children's shows were easier for me to understand. My goal was to be really good in English by the time my visa expired and I had to return to Italy.

Maria's boyfriend George came home on a one week leave during the summer. While he was home, he and Maria had an intense relationship. They acted like they were madly in love with each other. A few nights I could hear them making love in the bedroom. I immediately thought of Brandon and wished he could have been there with me. I would pull the covers over my head and try not to think about what was going on in the other room.

They would also argue with the same intensity. Sometimes, when the yelling got loud, I would go into Corey's room and make sure he wasn't hearing the fight. Sometimes he did hear and got scared. I would hold him and sing Italian songs to calm him.

In the mornings Maria and I were used to speaking to each other in Italian over breakfast. My English was getting better, but I was much more comfortable in Italian. When George was home, he got annoyed by that. He hadn't learned enough Italian to follow what we were saying.

"You know, that's rude," he said one day when he entered the kitchen and poured himself a cup of coffee.

"Don't worry, we're not talking about you," Maria said.

She winked at me and I giggled.

"Yeah, right," George said. He looked at me suspiciously. Then he turned back to Maria. "It's still rude."

"Give Luisa a break. She's still learning English."

"She's not going to learn it by speaking Italian."

"No. I speak English," I said. And to prove it I said, "How are you? How is your night?"

"See?" he said, glaring at Maria. "Is that so hard?" He turned to me. "I'm fine."

"Good," I said. "How long you stay here now?"

Before he could answer, Maria blew out a breath of exasperation, left the table and brought her coffee cup to the sink. I guessed why she was upset. She didn't like him being away.

"Unfortunately I have to leave again tomorrow," he said to me but he was looking over at Maria. "I can't help it, you know." He was talking to her now, not me. "What do you want me to do? If I don't go back, I get court-martialed."

"How about get a different job?"

"It doesn't work that way. I have to stay until my enlistment period is up. But then what? I still need a job. This is my job."

"You can find a different job."

"Good jobs don't grow on trees."

"Good jobs don't take you away from home most of the time, either," Maria said.

"Do we really have to argue about this again this morning? God!"

"Who's arguing? Luisa, am I arguing?" She turned back to George. "You're the only one arguing," she said. "You're always in a bad mood. I should be the one in a bad mood."

"What the hell is that supposed to mean?"

Just then I noticed Corey appear from the hallway and enter the kitchen. The loud voices and angry tone stopped him in his tracks. He stared at the two of them. Seeing them arguing darkened his face. He didn't do well with conflict. It scared him.

I jumped up and rushed over.

"Good morning, Mr. Corey," I said, hugging him as I always did. "Ready for breakfast? I make you eggs today, yes?"

He didn't answer, but instead stared at Maria and George.

"Is nothing," I told him. "Mamma and Papa is only excited about something."

"Papa?" Corey said.

George glared at me as well.

"Uh, Mamma and George," I said. When I got nervous, and their fights made me nervous, I made stupid mistakes like that.

George wasn't Corey's father. Maria had had him with a different man. She'd told me about him during one the many nights that George wasn't there. I think that George knew she'd told me about him, and that was another thing that he didn't like.

To be honest, to see George with Corey, you would never think he was Corey's father. He wasn't affectionate toward the boy. I never knew if it was because of Corey's illness or because George didn't know how to relate to children in general or perhaps because Corey was some other man's child and everything that that implied was something he struggled with.

Why he didn't like me very much, I wasn't so sure about until one night when he was away and Maria, Corey and I watched a movie together in their bedroom. Corey fell asleep before it ended. Maria decided to let him sleep there with her instead of bring him to his room. She did this often when George was away. She didn't like to sleep alone. Neither did I.

Maria and I had similar situations. Both our men were away most of the time. Many times I talked to her about how much I missed Brandon. This night she said why didn't I just stay and sleep with her and Corey. That way neither of us would be alone.

I truly didn't like sleeping alone. In Italy I didn't mind. But it was different here. I was in a strange country. I missed my family. I started to feel isolated and welcomed the chance to be with someone. So I agreed. I went to my room and put on my sweats for sleeping and cleaned up for bed.

When I got back to Maria's room, I could hear her in the bathroom, brushing her teeth. Corey was asleep on one side of the bed. I climbed in under the sheets in the middle of Maria and George's king-sized bed. A few minutes later, I heard the water in the bathroom stop and the door open. I looked up to see Maria coming out, dressed in the tiniest, silk lingerie.

I didn't know what to say, what to do. My first thought was to connect her invitation for me to sleep there with the way she was dressed. And that freaked me out. I liked Maria but not *that* way. I had no interest in women, any women. I wondered if I had done something to lead her to think differently.

But then I convinced myself that I was letting my imagination get away from me. Maria wouldn't try to lure me into her bed for sexual reasons with her son here beside us. She was a free spirit. She did her own thing. The sexy lingerie was probably just what she liked to wear and had nothing to do with my being here tonight.

"Corey is still asleep?" she asked as she slid in next to me.

"He must have been exhausted," I said.

"He really loves you, you know," she told me.

"I love him like he was my own."

"You're really good with him. Someday when you have your own, they're going to be lucky children."

"I don't think that's going to happen."

"Why not? You would make such a great mother."

"I don't know," I said.

The phone rang. It was almost midnight.

"That's got to be George," Maria said. She answered it, and she was right, it was George. They talked for a moment, and then Maria said, "Really, that's great!"

I looked at her and mouthed *Che cosa?* What?

"He's being transferred to San Diego," she said.

That was good. He would be closer. I wasn't sure how far San Diego was, but maybe he would live here. I was happy for my friend.

"I'm just here with Luisa," Maria said into the phone. He must have asked who she was talking to.

She was silent a moment, listening to him, then she smiled at me and answered him. "In bed, why?" She covered her mouth and laughed. She was enjoying teasing him. I didn't think that was such a good idea.

"We were watching a movie together," she said. "Why are you asking?"

She giggled again then looked at me and smiled, as though I were in on this with her. This whole thing made me uncomfortable. He already didn't like me much. This wasn't going to help.

"Do you want to say goodnight to her?" Maria asked.

Obviously he said no.

"Okay. I hope everything is good there," she said. "Here, it's really a hot night." She snickered silently, constantly looking over at me as though I were part of this. "Can't wear much, it's too uncomfortable."

I heard the low buzz of his voice from the receiver in her hand. I couldn't tell what he was saying, but he sounded angry.

Maria looked satisfied, as though she had achieved what she set out to do. "No, I'm fine. And if I need anything, I have Luisa here. Anything," she repeated.

She hung up and laughed out loud.

"Why do you do that to him?" I asked.

"It's so easy to get him going."

"You shouldn't try to make him jealous."

She waved off my concern. "Men should be jealous. They'll appreciate you more. And it's fun, too. You have to have fun, right?"

"He really thinks you and I would do something together? That's crazy."

"Well..." she said.

The way she said it I knew there was a lot more unsaid. She reached over and turned off the lamp, thrusting the room into darkness.

"There was one time," she said after a moment, "when I, you know, had some fun with a woman."

I didn't know what to say. I remained silent in the darkness. Corey was on the other side of me. I felt weird.

"But it was just physical," Maria said. "Not a relationship, you know. I didn't think that it meant anything. Don't get me wrong, the sex part was awesome, but I like men better. George shouldn't be insecure."

"If you tease him like that, he's going to be insecure."

"Jealous, not insecure. And like I said, a little jealousy is good for a relationship."

"I don't know about that."

"I do." She rolled over and said, "Good night, Luisa."

"Good night."

· · · · ·

In the middle of the night, I was startled from sleep by the sensation of being held. I opened my eyes and saw Maria snuggled up close to me. She had her arm around me. At first I thought she was awake and coming on to me, but then I saw that her eyes were closed and she was asleep. I gently reached over, lifted her arm off and eased it back to her side.

A while later I was awakened again by her arm around me and her body pressed against mine. If she had been awake, I would have jumped out of bed for and run. But she was asleep. I decided she was dreaming, probably about George—hopefully about George—but it still made me uncomfortable. I lifted her arm off me again and put it beside her and I slithered as far away as I could get without pushing Corey off the side of the bed. I had difficulty falling asleep again, worrying that she was going to move in on me again.

When the morning came, I woke up first and went to the kitchen for coffee. She got up a little later and joined me. She was still in her lingerie. She didn't say anything about what had happened during the night.

I had to ask her. "Maria, last night, did you have dreams about George?"

She looked at me oddly. "Why do you ask that?"

"In the middle of the night, you, uh, you kind of hugged me."

"Really?"

"Twice."

"I did?" And then she smiled.

I realized that she knew exactly what had happened last night. But I wasn't upset with her. She liked to have fun. That's all it was. She could have tried something, but she hadn't. That part of my life was kept for the weekends and for Brandon.

The next weekend, when Brandon came to Los Angeles, we went again to a motel. It was during the forty-eight hours of each weekend that I felt happiest. I had come halfway around the world for this man. The more time I spent with him, the more I realized how right my decision to come here had been.

And still hanging over it all was Brandon's unanswered question to me, his proposal. Would I marry him? Thinking about how I would answer him was going to be scary.

CHAPTER 10

As my summer in Los Angeles drew to an end, Corey, who was fine, started school. There was less for me to do around the house during the day, which meant more time to think. And the thing that I thought about the most was the expiration of my visa. By mid-October I would have to return to Italy. I'd had two wonderful months here, the weekends with Brandon being the best part. But I also enjoyed the time with Maria and Corey.

And I found the United States fascinating. People here seemed somehow freer than in Italy. I couldn't quite understand why, where that feeling came from. Maybe it was because everyone did whatever they liked as far as fashion and jobs and everything else, and people moved around a lot. They weren't restrained by a long history, obligation, and expectations.

In Italy, generations lived in the same place. Opportunity was limited. And everyone knew your business. The anonymity here gave you a kind of freedom.

The shallow roots allowed everyone to build their own lives however and wherever they wished. And afterwards, if that didn't suit you, you could rebuild again, somewhere else, in some other way. That intrigued me.

But to have that, I had to let go of the safety and comfort of having generations of family with me, the stability of knowing I was in a place where I belonged, the effortlessness of familiar surroundings, familiar customs. My home, my family, my beach, my markets, my friends, my everything was there. Here, I had nothing.

Except Brandon.

And a blank page upon which to write my own story, Luisa's life. I had too much free time to ponder this question.

* * * * *

Brandon had a long weekend in early September, for the Labor Day holiday, which gave us an extra day and night to spend together in the motel. We made love three or four times each day. Brandon always wanted desperately to give me pleasure, and he seemed never to be able to get enough. I felt the same way. Maybe because of those five days each week when we were apart, we wanted each so desperately when we were together. Whatever the reason, the sex was wonderful.

He showed me more of the city. We walked down Hollywood Boulevard and read the names of famous actors on the sidewalks. Brandon took me dancing. When I saw something in a store window, he bought it for me. He spent all his money on me. He took me to a beautiful restaurant where we sat outside and had a view of the Hollywood sign in the hills. The night was so perfect, I didn't want it ever to end. But it only reminded me that I was living in a temporary state and my time was quickly running out.

"I hate to leave," I said to him.

"Then don't leave."

"My visa expires soon."

"You can stay. Marry me and it won't matter that your visa expires."

"Is not so easy."

"Yes it is. Just say yes, you'll marry me. I don't want you to leave, Luisa. I don't ever want to be away from you. Going back to Twenty-nine Palms every Sunday night is hard enough, facing a whole week without you. I want to be with you, every day."

"I love being with you, too."

"Then marry me. Stay and marry me."

I took a breath and stared at the Hollywood sign for moment. I said, "I can't."

"Why not?"

"I have a responsibility in Italy. I promised my mother I would take care of the family."

He grasped my hands and looked into my eyes. "I want to marry you, Luisa."

"No, you don't," I said, my deep feelings finally coming out.

He looked stunned. "What?"

"You don't know what you're saying."

"Yes, I do. I'm saying I want you to marry me. I want you to spend the rest of your life with me. I know exactly what I'm saying. I know exactly what I want. You."

My insecurities about him, about men in general, about my obligations to my family, left me confused about what to do.

"Well," I said. "I can't answer right now. My mother said take care of the family."

"Forever?"

"No, but while they need me, yes."

"I need you," Brandon said.

Maybe he wanted me. But he didn't need me.

"I need time to decide," I told him.

He wrapped his strong arms around me and pulled me close. I closed my eyes and sank into the security of his chest.

"Please say yes," he whispered in my ear.

I remembered the first night I had met him, the night he asked me to dance. He'd said almost the same thing, please say yes. The sincerity in his voice went right to my heart. It would have been so much easier if I knew he was another Nino, if I could honestly say that he didn't really love me.

. . . . .

After Brandon had gone back to the base, I was in the living with Maria one evening. She was preparing for George to come back in a few days. We had a little wine to celebrate after Corey went to bed. I told her about my conversation with Brandon.

"I don't know what to do," I said. "Maybe it's not, you know, the best thing to do."

She leaned forward on the sofa and glared at me. "What's the matter with you, Luisa?"

"What do you mean?"

"Are you blind? Everybody can see. You can't?"

"See what?"

"When Brandon's here, he never takes his eyes off of you. He drives hours every weekend to be with you. He spends all of his money on you, and the Marines don't pay him much. Believe me, I know. But he spends it all on you. He begged you to come here. He bought you a ticket. He took you to meet his family. He loves you."

"I know, but..." My words trailed off. I didn't know what to say.

"No, no. Listen to me. He *really* loves you."

I wanted so badly to believe that. But it was difficult.

"What else do you want, Luisa?" she asked.

"I promised my mother that..."

"Oh, stop it," she said. I had told her that before. She waved her hand, dismissing what I was saying. "He loves you. But you're afraid. All the rest is nonsense."

"Yes, I'm afraid. What if it's a mistake to marry him?"

"What if it's a mistake not to?" she said.

"I know! It's hard to know what to do!"

"Follow your heart, that's what you do."

"My heart is in two places."

She threw up her hands, frustrated. "Listen, Luisa. A love like what you and he have doesn't come along often in life. Maybe only once. You let it go, you're going to regret it forever. Is that what you want?"

"Of course that's not what I want."

"Then marry him. I mean it. Marry him, or I swear to God, Luisa, I'll tell George to stay in Naples and I'll marry Brandon myself."

We laughed and hugged and while I was still scared to death of the decision, I was thankful that I had Maria to talk to.

· · · · ·

The next weekend, when Brandon came down from Twenty-nine Palms, I walked outside to the driveway to greet him. As I approached the car, I felt the heat from the motor after the two hour drive. Brandon opened the door and climbed out.

"Wow, what a sight to arrive to," he said, gazing at me. He hugged me. His strength, the scent of his body, the sound of his voice, it felt like coming home.

"I'll marry you," I said.

My words caught him off guard. For an instant, he looked confused. Then it registered. His face stretched into a huge grin and he scooped me off of the ground and into his arms, as through I weighed nothing at all.

"Yes!" she shouted, his voice echoing down the street and through the neighborhood. "Ooh-rah!"

In that moment, safe in his arms, I knew I had made the right decision.

· · · · ·

The next Friday, on September 17, in the same wedding chapel that Elizabeth Taylor had married one of her husbands, Brandon and I, and Maria, George and Corey waited in the anteroom for them to call us in. From there, I could hear the faint murmur of the Justice of the Peace performing the ceremony for another couple.

I was nervous. Brandon held my hand. I looked into his eyes and saw how happy he was. I, too, was happy, in spite of my nervousness. This wasn't the way I'd always seen myself getting married, by a Justice of the Peace in a secular chapel, but I loved Brandon and he loved me and this was the only way for me to stay. What we were doing was right.

I hadn't brought clothes for a wedding, and we didn't have time to buy any, so I wore the ivory linen shorts I'd brought along with an ivory jacket. Brandon had on white Levis and a navy blue silk shirt. He looked as sexy in that as any other man in a tuxedo. Corey, too, had white pants and a blue shirt, but he also had suspenders and he looked so cute, like a tiny grownup. Brandon and I asked Maria if Corey could be our ring bearer.

Brandon checked his watch. It was almost time. He squeezed my hand and smiled at me. Then he knelt down in front of Corey.

"Okay, champ. Do you remember what I need you to do?"

"Yes, sir."

"Carry the rings in both hands, stand by my left leg. When I turn to you and wink, you hand me the ring. Got it?"

"Got it, sir."

"Let's practice."

Brandon and I stood at one side of the room. Maria and Corey at the other. George sat and watched. Brandon smiled at Corey and said, "Go."

Corey held out his cupped hands in front of him, as though he were carrying water. In them he had the two rings. He walked slowly toward us. I saw by his face that he was nervous. He glanced over his shoulder at his mother behind him. Maria nodded and smiled. Then he turned back toward us and began to walk a little faster, but somehow one foot caught the other and he stumbled forward. The rings flew. Brandon lunged to catch Corey so he wouldn't hurt himself. He didn't get there before Corey hit the floor, but he quickly scooped him up and checked to make sure he wasn't hurt.

"Are you all right, champ?" Brandon asked.

I rushed toward them too.

"I'm okay," Corey said, his voice quiet and embarrassed.

"No harm, no foul," Brandon said. "Don't worry about it."

"Yeah, is no problem," I said, coming over, and when I did, I accidentally stepped on one of the rings.

I knelt down to pick it up. It was my ring, and it was bent. "Oh, my God."

"What's wrong?" Brandon asked.

I held it up for him to see. The ring was French style, very thin, and because it was eighteen carat gold it was soft, so when my heel had come down on it, the gold bent.

Just then the door opened up and the Justice of the Peace's assistant, a woman with a lot of make-up, cardboard stiff hair, and a bright red dress poked her hair out. "It's your turn," she said, almost singing the words, grinning the whole time.

"One second," Brandon said. He took the ring and quickly tried to squeeze it back into shape. It wasn't working.

"Is okay," I said. "Is not matter."

"Are you ready?" the grinning woman sang.

"Ready!" Brandon said. He took my hand. "Let's do this, my love."

· · · · ·

Brandon stood at the front with the Justice of the Peace, an older man with coal black hair. I couldn't tell if it was a toupee or dyed. He had long sideburns, the way Elvis Presley used to wear his, and a black tuxedo that looked out of place the way the rest of us were dressed. But other couples did come in gown and tux, so I assumed he had to be ready for anything.

Maria and George sat in the front row, close behind Brandon. Corey stood behind me, the smiling assistant to the Justice of the peace holding his hand. The Justice of the Peace nodded to the smiling woman. She pressed a button on the wall, turning on a recording of the wedding march, and then told me to go ahead and make my way slowly up to Brandon.

It felt strange to force myself to walk at this unusual pace. The whole time I just wanted to hurry and get there. When I finally reached the front, I grasped Brandon's hand. We both looked at each other. I felt so nervous now that I was struggling to breathe. I turned and looked at the Justice of the Peace. He smiled at me then nodded to the woman at the back. She pushed Corey toward us.

I thought she better be careful or he might trip again and lose the ring, but he walked up the aisle toward us, at a slow and steady pace. His face was set in a serious look. He reached us without falling and stood confidently beside Brandon. Brandon looked down at him and gave a proud nod. Corey nodded back. Maria, who had walked down the aisle and was now standing in the first row of seats, looked like she might cry. The smiling woman stood off to the side. The rest of the chapel was empty.

I turned back to the Justice of the Peace.

"We are gathered here today…" he began. The rest was a blur to me. I was trying to digest what I was doing. I was getting married and my family wasn't here. I hadn't even told my father. Is this how my mother would have wanted it? Is this really the way I wanted it? I had come here telling myself that it was the right thing to do. My doubts now were just jitteriness. I reminded myself that I had debated it all before. This is where I should be. This is what I should be doing.

"Brandon Cloutier," the Justice of the Peace said, yanking my attention back to the wedding happening around me. "Do you take Luisa La Rotonda to be your lawfully wed wife…"

"I do," he said.

"Wait," the Justice of the Peace said. "I'm not finished."

"Sorry. Go ahead."

"To have and to hold, from this day forward, through richer and poorer, in sickness and in health, until death do you part?"

"Absolutely I do." Brandon turned to me and smiled, looking filled with joy. He squeezed my hand. I saw in his eyes that he did love me.

The Justice of the Peace spoke to me now. "Luisa La Rotonda," he said. "Do you take Brandon Cloutier to be your lawfully-wed husband? To have and to hold…"

The rest of his words faded out. I just stared at Brandon. I didn't understand everything that the Justice of the Peace had been saying, to Brandon or to me, partly because of my English, partly because I was nervous. But I understood that what he was saying would result in my being married to Brandon when this was done. Once this was finished, that was it. I had to be certain. For me, marriage was for life. This would be forever. I looked up into Brandon's eyes, hoping that I was reading him right, that he was, as I believed, the right man for me.

I realized now that everyone was silent and looking at me. I wasn't sure what to do.

Brandon grasped my other hand. Now he was holding both my hands. He squeezed them a little and leaned closer to me. "Luisa," he said, "do you love me?"

"Yes."

"Do you want to marry me?"

I took a breath. "Yes."

He smiled. "Then you have to tell the man."

I turned to the Justice of the Peace.

He said, "Luisa La Rotonda, do you take Brandon Cloutier to be your lawfully-wed husband, to have and to hold from this day forward, through richer and poorer, in sickness in health, until death do you part?"

The Justice of the Peace spoke the words a little too quickly. I didn't understand it all, particularly the last part. I turned toward him and repeated what I'd heard, "Until they do your part?"

"No, no, death," the Justice of the Peace repeated, pronouncing each word slowly and clearly, "death...do...you...part."

The word "death" made the whole thing sound terrible. It reminded me of my mother. Of the horrible relationship she and my father had. Was that what I was getting myself into?

Brandon must have seen the anguish in my face because he squeezed my hands again to get my attention and said, "Until forever. Do you take me until forever?"

That I understood. That had only positive connotations. I looked straight at him, being very serious, and said, "Yes, I do."

The Justice of the Peace turned to Brandon. "Do you have the rings?"

Brandon looked down at Corey and winked. Corey raised his cupped hands with the two rings. Brandon took the bent ring. I took his. He held my left hand and struggled to put the bent ring on my finger, repeating what the Justice of the Peace told him.

"With this ring, I thee wed..."

The only thing that mattered at the moment was that my heart was filled with joy. This was the happiest day of my twenty-four years of life.

I put Brandon's ring on him.

"I now pronounce you husband and wife," the Justice of the Peace said. He told Brandon to kiss me.

Brandon pulled me closer and kissed me with so much passion that all of my nervousness disappeared and I felt eager to begin the next phase of my life, as Luisa Cloutier.

From the seats, George shouted, "Ooh-rah!"

CHAPTER 11

Brandon took the marriage license to the base and applied for us to get housing together now that we were husband and wife. We had to wait, but Brandon promised it wouldn't be too long. Until then we agreed that I would stay with Maria and George. Things were different with George staying there. Maria asked me to speak to her only in English when George was around.

"He still thinks we're talking about him?" I asked.

"It just makes him uncomfortable. Just try to speak English when he's around."

I did as Maria asked. It wasn't a big problem. The more time I spent in the U.S., the better my English was getting. I just thought it was stupid for him to be suspicious of us. Maria loved him. Why else would she stay with a man who was away so much? Her love for him was clear, even though they still fought a lot. Many nights I heard them arguing in their room. Often I'd go and take Corey to a different part of the house so he wouldn't have to hear them yelling. But there were just as many other nights I heard them making love and distracted Corey so he wouldn't hear that either.

George also kept asking me if Brandon had heard from the Marine Corps yet regarding housing. It was clear he preferred me to leave. If I had had someplace else to go, I would have. Every time Brandon came down to LA to visit me or whenever he called, I asked him when "our home" would be ready.

"Not much longer, my love. Just hang on."

One evening I was in my room studying my English-Italian dictionary. I heard Maria and George start yelling at each other. Here they go again, I thought. It always started out kind of low, just loud enough that I could hear their most heated statements, and then it would fade again. Sometimes it stayed at this level until they finished. Other times it would flare up even louder. This night it got really loud. I heard both their voices screaming. I couldn't make out exactly what they were saying, but it was clear that it was a bunch of angry outbursts.

Amid the yelling I heard a thumping sound and I heard Corey start to cry. He must have fallen. I hurried out into the hallway and I started toward his room, but then I realized that his cries were coming from the opposite direction, from where Maria and George were fighting. I turned and went to their door. Corey was still crying inside. George yelled something and I thought I heard him shout "*Shut up!*"

Without thinking, I knocked on the door. I was worried about Corey, who was still crying. And George's yelling also scared me. Some Marines, not Brandon, but some others, had bad tempers. I'd seen it in Italy. I didn't know George well enough to know what he was capable of, but I already knew that I annoyed him.

The door flung open so suddenly it startled me. Maria filled the opening. The first thing I noticed was that she had Corey in her arms. She thrust him toward me. "*Guardalo!*" she said, imploring me to watch him. She barely had a voice after all the screaming. I struggled to grab him. He wrapped his arms around me and held tightly, still crying.

"What's happening?" I asked.

Maria didn't answer. As she started to go back inside the bedroom and close the door, I got a look at her face.

Her left eye was swollen and bruised. A streak of blood went from a cut on her lip, down her chin and onto her shirt. Her teeth were also red with blood. Her eyes were wild with fear. The door closed in front of me before I could say or do anything.

My first thought was that I wanted Brandon here to protect me and her and Corey. But he was two hours away. I needed to call the police. With Corey in my arms I rushed up the hallway to the kitchen. I grabbed the phone. To call the police you dialed 9-1-1. That I had learned early on. I started to dial when a hand grabbed my wrist and pulled my arm away from the phone. I spun around to see George glaring at me. He was breathing heavily, his face bright red with anger. With his other hand he pulled the phone away from me.

"You're not calling anyone!" he shouted.

"No, no. Is okay. I don't call no one," I said. I feared what he might do to me and Corey. "Is okay. No problem." I wanted to calm him down, but I saw it wasn't working.

"This is between Maria and me," he shouted. "Just stay out of it, do you hear?"

I nodded, holding tightly to Corey.

His outburst had frightened Corey even more. The little boy held tighter to me and buried his face in my shirt to muffle his crying.

"You scaring him," I said.

"Shut up!" he yelled at Corey, leaning closer to him, yelling in his ear.

I pulled Corey away and moved around to the other side of the table. "Is okay. I'll have him stop."

"Do that!" he yelled. "Just go back to your room and stay there."

I nodded again.

With the phone receiver still in his hand, he turned around and stormed back up the hallway toward his and Maria's room. As soon as he closed the bedroom door behind him, I ran to my room, still carrying Corey. I prayed to God he didn't do anything else to Maria. The only other phone was in Maria's bedroom. I couldn't even call for help.

The yelling resumed. I heard both of their voices. Something smashed. Corey was terrified. We sat in the corner in the dark holding each other. After some time, the fight went out into the hallway. I heard doors slamming and both of them in the hallway outside my room.

"Get out and find yourself somewhere else to stay!" Maria said.

"Go fuck yourself!" George replied. "I don't need you or this place."

"Then go! Get out!"

"I'm going!"

"Go!"

"I am, so shut the fuck up!"

"You shut the fuck up!"

I heard him stomp down the hall and through the kitchen and I heard the back door slam shut. Faintly, outside, a car engine started, followed by tires squealing. A moment later my bedroom opened and Maria came in.

"Are you two all right?" she asked, struggling between sobs.

We both ran over to hug her.

· · · · ·

While I was holding a towel over the cut on her lip to stop the bleeding, I said, "Maria, this is not okay. You can't allow him to do this. To you or to Corey."

She winced from the pain on her lip. "I know," she whispered.

"You have to call the police," I said.

"I know. You'll help me?" she said.

"Of course I will."

I sat with her and held her hand while she called 911 and talked to the police. When she told them that George had left, they told her to come down to the police station to make a report. I went with her. We dropped Corey off at the house of one of Maria's friends and then went to the station. They said we needed to talk to a detective and they had us wait. Hours passed. Maria kept going back to the window, asking how much longer. They would always answer, "We've got a lot of cases, lady. You just have to wait your turn."

After almost three hours, Maria stood up. "That's it. Let's go. I'm not waiting any longer."

"We have to make the report," I said.

"They're not going to do anything anyway." Switching to English so the police would hear her, she said, "The police don't do anything for women victims of domestic violence." Then she said to me, "Let's go."

I knew that something had to be done about George to make sure he didn't go back there, and I could see the frustration on Maria's face, but she was right, the police didn't seem to care.

"George isn't going to do anything," Maria told me in the car as we drove to pick up Corey.

"I don't trust him."

"I'm not letting him come back, that's for sure, but he's not the type of man to try to break in and do anything to me, don't worry."

"I do worry," I said.

"I know him. He can be a jerk, but he's not a criminal."

"Look at your lip, Maria. He did that."

She was silent for a moment, peering at herself in the rearview mirror. Finally she said, "It'll be okay."

· · · · ·

I barely slept the next night, fearing that George would come back. When Brandon arrived for his weekend visit, I told him what had happened and that I was afraid George would return. Brandon tried to talk Maria into getting a restraining order against George. She kept insisting that it wasn't necessary. And anyway, she said, the paper wouldn't keep him away from the house if he wanted to come there. It wouldn't make anyone safer. It would only give her recourse if he did decide to come to the house.

When we got to the motel, Brandon hugged me and kissed my forehead and told me that he didn't feel good about my staying any longer with Maria.

"I can't force her to get a restraining order," he said, "but, my love, I promise I'm going to get you out of there."

When he went back to the base the next week, he pushed the Marines harder to give us a house of our own in Twenty-nine Palms. Until then he found a place for me to stay in Torrance, just outside Los Angeles. The friend of a friend had two daughters, Melissa and Nicole, and she needed someone to help her take care of the kids. Leaving Maria and Corey was difficult. We all cried. I'd grown close to Corey and hated saying goodbye. But I knew it was for the best.

During the months living in Torrance, the kids and I grew attached to each other, just as I'd grown attached to Corey. Finally in March, Brandon called with the good news. The Marines had a house for us in Twentynine Palms. Leaving these kids, too, was difficult and heartbreaking, but I knew that it was time for Brandon and me to begin living our lives as normal husbands and wives, together in the same house. So, tears in my eyes, I said goodbye to my other family and drove out to the desert with Brandon, filled with expectations of what lay ahead and relief that we would never have to be apart again.

CHAPTER 12

The Marine Corps base at Twenty-nine Palms is surrounded by the Mojave Desert. I had never been in such a location before. It was like entering a completely different world. Instead of grass and plants in our back yard, we had sand and cactus. The heat was extreme. I always loved it hot, but Brandon suffered as summer dragged on and the temperature remained over 100 degrees most of the daylight hours. The house the Marines gave us didn't have central air, and even at night it was so hot that sleeping was uncomfortable.

To escape, we would drive to Palm Springs over the weekend and get a hotel with A/C and a pool. Sometimes we'd meet friends there, another couple we had known from when Brandon had been stationed in Italy. We also spent a lot time at Joshua Tree National Park, hiking, enjoying nature, climbing on the unusual desert rock formations. I saw my first coyote there. Brandon told me to stay in the car while he got out to take a picture. He was always worried about my safety.

I was so happy to be living with him, and so thankful for all the things he did for me. He worked hard every day. We had to straighten out my immigration, because getting married hadn't automatically made me a legal resident and we found out I was here illegally. He paid a lawyer thousands of dollars to work on my immigration. He took a second job at Little Caesar's Pizza in order to help make ends meet. Many nights he came home exhausted.

I started falling into the role I'd had in Italy after my mother died. I cleaned the house and cooked for Brandon every day. He loved coming home to a hot meal. As tired as he was at the end of the day, he always had the energy to make love. Some days we'd make love before he left for work and then again after he came home. If the custom here had been like in Italy and he'd have come home for lunch, we would have made love then too. We were both so excited to be together, no longer just on the weekends.

Part of his training involved him going away for days at a time. The first time it happened, I had only been at Twenty-nine Palms for a month or so. He said he had to go overnight bivouac in the desert.

"What's that?" I asked.

"It's like camping, but without a tent. We make shelter from whatever we can find."

"Why?"

"So we'll be prepared if it ever happens in a deployment."

"And me?"

He smiled and hugged me. "You can't come, my love."

"I know. But I'm going to be alone here?"

"You'll be fine. It's safe here. You're surrounded by Marines. No one's going to do anything. I promise."

I wanted to believe him, but when night fell, my fears rose. The desert became black when the sun went down. Scary sounds echoed from outside, strange animal howls, wind scratching over the sand, the house itself settling and making noises. Everything seemed so open and vulnerable there compared to Italy.

Before going to bed, I went to the kitchen, took the largest knife I found, and brought it to bed with me. I slid it under the pillow and placed my hand on it and kept it in my grip until I fell asleep.

In the morning my fear gave way to loneliness and nostalgia for my family in Italy. How often was this going to be how I lived? I understood that it was his job and he had to do it, but this wasn't something I liked at all. I had moved countries, left everything I knew behind, but not to be left alone in a strange place. I wanted to be with my husband, my love.

When Brandon returned home and took me straight to bed to make up for the lost night, he found the knife still under the pillow.

"What happened here?" he said. "Were you cooking in the bedroom?"

"For protection," I said.

"I told you there's nothing you need protection from here. You're safe. Do you think I would leave you alone if I thought you weren't?"

"I'm just not used to it. It makes me miss home. I want to see my family, Brandon."

"I understand. But you can't go back until we fix your immigration status or else you might not be able to come back into the country."

"I hate this."

He wrapped his arms around me and held me tightly. I felt protected, safe.

"I know how you feel," he said. "I felt the same way when I joined the Marines and had to leave home for the first time. It's always hard to leave your family. But it's part of becoming an adult. Our parents left their homes in order to make their own. That's what we're doing."

"Left, but not forever."

"No, and you haven't left forever either. I promise you, once your status is legal, I'll buy you a ticket to go to home to Italy. I promise. You just have to wait a little longer. I'm doing everything I can to get it straightened out."

"I know you are."

I knew he was trying. Whatever I wanted, he always tried to make sure I had it. Because of the way he treated me, every day I woke up feeling loved.

Some evenings we would just drive out to Joshua Tree, park the car overlooking the rocks and the desert, and sit with the window open and the cool night breeze blowing through, and we'd talk. One night I told Brandon that I wanted to earn money and contribute to the household. He worked two jobs. I stayed home all the time.

"You don't need to work," he said. "I'll take care of earning the money."

"I still want to try to get a job," I said. "I need to get out of the house, talk to people."

"Luisa, my love, I want you to do whatever will make you happy, but I don't want you to feel like you *have to* work. Earning a living is my responsibility. Not yours."

I hugged him and peered up into his sincere eyes. "I know you can make enough money for us. But I always worked...before my mother died."

"But now you're with me. I'll work. You should do something you like."

"I like to work."

He laughed. "Something else you like."

"It will help me learn English to speak to more people."

"You speak very well. I understand everything you say."

"But *I* don't understand everything *you* say."

He leaned over, put his hands on my face and kissed me passionately. I was caught by surprise, but I loved it. When he moved away, it took me a moment to breathe again.

"You understood that, didn't you?" he said.

I smiled at him. "Yes."

"Okay then."

I realized it was important to him that I didn't work, so I accepted it for then. But I did want a career. I couldn't picture myself staying home every day, the way I'd done after my mother died, the way my mother had. That wasn't for me. That wouldn't give me a happy life.

. . . . .

I found myself alone a lot. Brandon left often for overnight exercises. And working two jobs, he wasn't around much. I hated sleeping alone. I hated eating alone. I even had to go to the hospital alone when I was stung by a scorpion while he was away.

When he was home, he was often tired from working so hard. The Marines were stressful and he needed time to unwind when he came home. But I needed time with him, and many times my need for his companionship conflicted with his need to de-stress from the day's work.

One time, when I was missing him terribly, he came home late from work. I had been anticipating his return and needed to be with him, to make love and feel like a couple. But when he walked in the door I was surprised to see that he had brought a buddy home from the base. He hadn't told me. Fortunately I'd made enough dinner. The three of us ate together, the two of them talking, me feeling like an outsider. After we ate, I thought Brandon was going to say goodnight to his friend and spend the rest of the night just him and me, but instead he and his friend went into the living room to play on the PlayStation.

I was so upset I could barely keep from throwing all of the dishes and glasses in the kitchen at him and his friend. I silently cleaned the kitchen and then went upstairs to our bedroom without saying a word. An hour passed before I heard the door, a car leaving the driveway, then Brandon's footsteps coming upstairs.

After he entered the bedroom, saying, "What a day!" he stopped, shocked to see my packed suitcases on the bed.

"What are you doing, Luisa?"

"I'm leaving."

"What's wrong?"

"I'm going home."

"Why? What's wrong? I don't get it."

"I don't want to be here anymore."

"Why?"

"I hate it here. I hate being alone. We're not married. You're never here. When you are, you play with your friend, you don't come to be with me. I had enough. *Basta!* I'm leaving!"

He rushed over to me and grasped my shoulders. "No, please Luisa, don't do this. I love you. I need you."

"No, you don't. You need PlayStation."

"No, no, I'm sorry. I was just trying to let go of stress. I didn't want to be grouchy with you, I wanted to get rid of all of that on the game. But I would much rather be with you. I'll never do it again. I promise you."

I calmed myself and stared up into his eyes. "I'm lonely here, Brandon. I miss my family. I don't have friends. I don't do anything worthwhile. I hate my life. I can't stay any longer."

"You can't leave me," he said. He dropped down to his knees. "Please, Luisa. I need you. If you leave, I—I—I couldn't stand it, losing you."

"What about me? I can't stand this."

"Then we'll change this. But you can't leave. I love you."

"I love you, too, Brandon."

"Then why do you want to leave?"

"I don't want to leave. I just can't live like this."

"Whatever you want, I'll do. Whatever changes it takes, we'll change it. But you have to stay."

"I need a life too," she said. "I need to work, and I need you here."

"Done," he said.

I pulled him up. I couldn't stand to see him on his knees. "I love you. I miss my family, but I love you more."

"And that's what matters. Our love for each other. As long as we're here for each other, we'll make it. It won't always be easy, but we can do it if we stay strong together. Can you do that? Stay strong with me."

"I can," I said.

"I'll be here for you, always. But you have to promise me that you won't leave me. I can't go to work every day, wondering if you'll be here when I come home or if you'll be gone. I can't live like that."

"I'll be here. I'll always be here."

He scooped me up into his arms the way he used to, took me to the bed and made passionate love all night. It was what I needed. I needed to know that he loved me and I could count on him because as long as I knew that, I could make it through anything with him.

. . . . .

I applied for a position at the officer's club on the base and was hired to work in the kitchen, cutting vegetables, making coleslaw, flipping burgers. It wasn't what I thought of as my life's work, as a career, but it was a start. I worked hard, never complained, was always on time. The manager said I was one of her best workers. She noticed how I did whatever was asked and learned every job in the kitchen. I was only there a couple weeks when she asked me if I wanted to come out of the kitchen and learn to make omelets and pancakes at the station in the dining room.

"Sure."

"Come at six am tomorrow," she said. "I'll put you on the breakfast line and see how that works out."

I was nervous now that I wasn't in the kitchen, but instead was out in the dining room at the omelet station. A line of officers waited for their made to order eggs. The manager did it first, to show me how. She was able to break the eggs with one hand and flip the omelet without even using a spatula. After she did a few, she then told me to take over.

"Onions and cheese, Ma'am," a Marine officer told me.

I broke the eggs using two hands, added the onions and cheese, let it cook for a minute or so. The manager, who watched over my shoulder the whole time, said "You can turn it now."

I picked up the spatula. Nothing fancy from me yet. When I tried to turn it over, the whole thing somehow slid out of the frying pan and splattered on the floor.

The officer laughed and said, "In-coming!"

I didn't understand what that meant. The other officers understood and they laughed too. The manager told me not to worry about it.

"Happens to everyone first time."

I started to give her the skillet to make the omelet, thinking I might be happier back inside the kitchen, but she gestured for me to try again.

"You can do it," she said.

The officer waiting smiled at me and said, "I'm in no rush, sweetheart. I don't deploy for another six months."

I broke two new eggs, added onions and cheese, and started cooking another omelet, determined to succeed this time. And I did. I handed the nearly perfect omelet to the officer and said, "Enjoy it."

"I'd enjoy it more if you came with it, pretty lady."

"Give her a break, will you?" the manager said.

"Hey, I'm a Marine first and foremost. I see a hot girl, I'm going to do something about it."

"Thank you," I said, "but I'm married."

"Don't worry, I'm not going to hold that against you."

The officer in line behind him said, "You struck out, Lieutenant. I suggest you move on."

The first officer went to sit down.

The one that told him to leave stood in front of me and smiled. "Good morning, Ma'am!"

"Good morning. What would you like?"

"I'll just have me a mushroom omelet and your phone number." He gestured toward the man he'd just sent away and said, "Why have a lieutenant when you can have a captain?"

* * * * *

The job wasn't perfect, but I liked that I was out and seeing people all the time. And I was earning a little money, which made our lives a little easier. Perhaps the best thing to come out of the job was that it proved to me that I could impress my boss in a different country and in a different language.

Though Brandon accepted my working, he didn't like it. He liked that I was happy. In the end, that's what mattered to him the most. When he found out that while I was working, other Marines were hitting on me, he went from not liking the job to hating it. What made matters worse was that the men hitting on me were officers and so he couldn't even talk to them and tell them to find someone else to pursue.

One day, while I was working at the pancake station, I looked up past the officers I was cooking for and saw Brandon walking across the dining room. As a corporal, he wasn't allowed in this place. The only thing I could think, watching in shock as he approached me, was that he was going to get into trouble. I'd learned from Italy and my experiences with Brandon on the base there that he sometimes acted impulsively when it came to me. I had gotten into trouble the time we made love in my car outside the gate. I didn't want to be the one causing him to get into trouble again.

He came straight over to me. The officers in the dining room didn't say anything. They must have assumed he worked there.

He arrived at my station and said, "Put the spatula down."

He caught me off guard. I didn't understand what was going on.

"Brandon," I whispered, "you can't be here."

"Put the spatula down," he repeated. His expression was neutral, Marine-like, the way they held themselves when they were in formation, so I couldn't tell if he was upset or not.

I put down the spatula and started to come around the cooking station so I could quietly convince him to leave. If they put him in the base jail as punishment, I would have to be without him again and didn't want that.

"Listen, you have to go..." I started to say.

Before I could finish, he grabbed me and lifted me in the air the way he'd done at the airport in Boston when I first arrived. He wasn't angry at all, but instead was filled with happiness.

"I'm getting out," he said.

"What?"

"I'm getting out of the Marines and we're leaving California."

This was all a surprise to me. It left me confused. "What do you mean?"

"I told them I'm not re-upping. I'm getting out and you and I are leaving here."

It was a surprise, but I knew it was something good. Brandon had long thought that the Marines wasn't for him, that he would do his four years and leave. He hadn't made his final decision until now, and with the decision made, I started to feel a little nervous. This was his steady, stable job. Once he was out, what would we have?

He put me down, and I took him over near the kitchen door to talk privately.

"Where are we going?" I asked.

"Massachusetts." He grinned.

He said we could stay temporarily with his mother, he would get a job there and we could make a good life. More than a year earlier I had decided that I loved Brandon enough to follow him anywhere. I had followed him to California. Massachusetts would be the next stop on our lives together. I trusted him and his confidence and I accepted that this was the right decision.

PART THREE

CHAPTER 13

We drove from Southern California to Massachusetts. I loved the days together, driving across the country, staying in little motels, making love every chance we got. We would be staying with Brandon's mother once we arrived and getting the chance to be intimate was going to be more difficult, we knew, so we wanted to take advantage of any chance we got before we arrived.

We stopped in Las Vegas and at the Grand Canyon. The two were as opposite as could be, but I found both of them amazing. Texas seemed to go on forever. New Orleans was a lot of fun. The trip was one of the best weeks Brandon and I had spent together. Nothing else to do but experience it together. No work or friends or problems getting in the way. If it were possible to spend your entire life driving around with the one you loved the most in life, that would be the best way to live life.

When we arrived in Massachusetts, everything was covered in snow, something I'd never experienced before in Italy, California or North Carolina. It was night, and as we drove though Hudson toward Brandon's mother's apartment, the streets were empty except for a plow roaring by, clearing a path on the opposite side of the road. Brandon had no problem driving in the snow. In fact, he seemed at ease, like he belonged here. Seeing his confidence and calmness, took away much of my anxiety.

Still, I couldn't help but wonder what was going to happen. Neither of us had job lined up. We'd saved a little money, but not enough to survive for more than a few weeks. We were starting again, something I'd been doing so much in the last few years. I longed for the day when I would feel settled, permanent. Still, being there felt right.

The night air was so harsh and icy when I got out to the car at

Brandon's mother's apartment building and walked toward the entrance that it felt like the cold was going to crack the bones in my face. When I'd visited here my first summer, it had been cold at night, but nothing like this. If it weren't for Brandon, if this hadn't been the town he came from, if he hadn't been hurrying through the cold right by my side, I would never have come to a place like this.

Finding your soul mate changes many things about you. Not only the things you do and places you go, but also the things you realize you *can* do, the difficulties you thought you could not surmount, but with that person they become bumps or turns in life's journey that you can go through and emerge from, a different and better person.

I was not the person who had met Brandon that night at the Marine dance in Napoli. All that we had experienced together—the good and the bad—had changed me and continued to shape me each and every day. I did not regret a moment of it, even the hardest times, because they had brought me to where I was that day, who I was that day. I hoped Brandon, too, had no regrets. When he held me, when he looked into my eyes, when he made love to me, I always felt that unyielding love of his. I needed him to continue feeling the same way, even as we both emerged different, shaped by our experiences.

. . . . .

It was not easy, starting again.

Brandon's mother had a one bedroom apartment. Brandon asked for sheets and a blanket to make up the sofa for us, but she insisted we take her bedroom.

"Two people can't fit on that sofa," she said.

"No," I said.

"Mom, we'll take the sofa," Brandon said. "It's not a problem."

"It is for me. This is my house. I say who sleeps where."

"I'm not going to take your bed," I told her.

"Yes you are," she said with a smile.

She insisted. She too was rebuilding her life, saving up to buy her own house. So she understood what it was like for us and she went out of her way to help. Brandon had told me about his childhood, about how his mother had run off with a man when he and his brother and sister were children. They'd had to live with his grandmother. It was traumatic for Brandon. I think it was traumatic for his mother, too. Helping Brandon when he was starting again after leaving the Marines must have given her some relief.

For Brandon, it was torture. He wanted to be self-sufficient, he wanted to give me a good life. He hated having to depend on his mother. Those few weeks he spent all of his days looking for work, but the economy wasn't so good up there and he struggled to find work. Our money ran out. I started looking in the newspaper for a job for me. I didn't want another waitress job. I wanted a job where I would be respected, be a professional, have the chance to grow, get promoted. I called all of the ads I found, but no one was offering to hire me, or even to have me come in for an interview. Maybe it was my accent. Maybe someone like me could only get work as a waitress. If I had to, I would, but I wanted to try for something better.

Brandon looked tortured because he hadn't found work. The winter didn't bother him, like it did me. In fact, he preferred it to the summer. But not being able to provide was killing him. I told him it would be okay, that things would turn around, but as time went by, we both were losing our optimism.

When he finally did get a job, it was as a security guard, earning minimum wage. But he was so relieved. It wasn't nearly enough money to live on, even for someone sleeping on their mother's sofa, but he was so thankful that he was earning it for himself. He cashed the first paycheck and gave me most of the money.

"Here, go shopping with this," he said. "Get what you need."

Then he gave his mom some money too, to help her with the expenses of the apartment.

I saw the positive change in his demeanor immediately. It was as if he felt like he was a man again.

"I'm going to do better than this," he told me that night as we lay awake on the sofa. "I'm going to get a better job, but at least we have money coming in."

"I know you will," I told him. I snuggled up close and caressed his chest. I wished we had our own place, somewhere we could be alone and make love whenever we wanted. We struggled together, and that made me feel closer to him. I knew we would get there, having our own home, living a better life. I believed in him. I just needed to have patience.

· · · · ·

I continued looking in the newspaper for a job. I had always wanted to work in a bank. When I was a child, Rodolfo and Angela and I used to pretend that I was a banker and they were customers coming in for money. We made some play *lira* with paper. My mother commented that I handled the play money better than the real tellers at the bank.

I saw an ad in the newspaper for a teller job at the Marlborough Savings Bank and decided to apply. The ad said to call Karla Digiulio in Human Resources. Her name was Italian so I thought that was good sign.

When I called, I got a voicemail and left a message. Then I sat by the phone and waited for her to call back. My mother-in-law came home late that afternoon and saw me sitting by the phone. I explained why.

"But she doesn't call me back," I said. "Maybe it was my accent, she didn't understand me."

"I'm sure she understood you. Don't worry, she'll call. She's probably very busy. Give her a little more time."

"You think so?"

"Yes. Now, did you make enough copies of your resume?" she asked.

"Resume? I don't have one. Oh, my god! What am I going to do?"

She sat down and patted me on the arm. "Don't worry. I'll help you."

She grabbed a note pad and a pen from a drawer in the kitchen and we sat at the table. "I'll print it from a computer at work," she said. "Okay, let's start with your education. Do you have any college at all? It doesn't have to be a degree, but any classes, anything?"

"No."

"That's okay. Not everyone has that. A high school diploma is good enough for this kind of job."

We then moved on to my work experience. She included the two waitress jobs I'd had in the U.S. and made it sound like I had gained customer service experience that would be helpful in the bank. When I told her about working for the construction company in Napoli, she typed that in and said I had been the office manager. When we finished, she took me to Staples to make copies. Next I had to wait for a call back.

The next week, when I still hadn't heard back, I asked my mother in law what I should do. "Do you think I should call Karla Digiulio again?" I said. "I don't want to annoy her."

"Why not call?" she said. "At this point it won't hurt? If she doesn't want you, then it doesn't matter if you annoy her. If she does want you, she'll be glad that you are eager and show your interest."

It made sense to me, so I called again and again got her voicemail.

"Hello, this is Luisa Cloutier," I said, trying to speak without an accent. "I called you last week and left a message. I wanted to tell you that I am really, really interested in the teller position you have in the newspaper. Can you call me back?" I gave her my mother in law's number then said, "Thank you."

I hung up and let out a long breath, relieved it was done.

"Good job," my mother in law said.

"Could you tell I had an accent?"

She smiled at me. "Barely." A short time later, Karla Digiulio called back. One of the first things she asked was, "Where's your accent from?"

· · · · ·

My interview was two days later. I spent the morning doing my hair and makeup, trying to make myself look my best. My blue and gold skirt and jacket were the most professional outfit I had. The high heels made me look taller, and I thought that would be good. I'd read somewhere that the taller you are, the better people think of you. I was determined to get this job.

Brandon let me take the car that morning. I drove to the main office in Marlborough. Everyone was very friendly. "Have a seat, Ms. Cloutier." "Ms. Digiulio will be right with you, Ms. Cloutier." "Can I get you anything while you're waiting, Ms. Cloutier?"

Karla Digiulio was the human resources manager. She greeted me with a smile and a handshake and thanked me for coming. I was overjoyed that they were interviewing me. We went into her office, where she gave me an application and asked me to fill it out. I did that. We talked awhile about my work experience and then she told me that I had to take a test.

"What kind of test?" I asked. I worried that it was a English grammar test or something like that.

"General aptitude," she said. "Math, some scenarios of things that might happen at the bank, that kind of thing. Just do your best."

I was nervous until I started taking the test. I knew most of the answers and felt that I did well. After I finished, Kathy thanked me and said they'd let me know. As days passed and I didn't hear from her, my confidence faded. Maybe I hadn't done so well on the test after all. Or maybe my accent was too heavy. Or maybe they didn't think my work experience was good enough. Or maybe they had called my school in Italy. I needed this job. Brandon was going to work every day, coming home exhausted. I was desperate to help out.

Finally the call came. "We'd like you to come for a second interview," Kathy told me.

"Yes, I will. Thank you."

When Brandon got home, I could barely wait until he got in the doorway.

"They want me to come back! The bank wants me to come back for another interview."

"Yes!" He wrapped his arms around me and lifted me into the air. "You got the job! That's great! Ooh-rah!"

"It's just a second interview."

He looked me in the eyes and said, "My love, you got the job. I know you got it. This interview is just a formality."

. . . . .

I started a week later. My boss was an assistant manager named Wilma. They were starting me at minimum wage. But it was a foot in the door.

This was the chance I needed. I would show them that I was worth more.

When I used to go to the bank in Italy for my work, I saw that customer service was horrible. People always had to wait in long lines for at least an hour to do anything there. When you finally got to the front, the teller usually had a nasty face and wasn't friendly at all. Sometimes they'd even be talking on the phone to their family or friends. My thinking was to do this job the way that I had wished they did it in Italy, to be fast, friendly, smile and not make careless mistakes.

And that's what I did. After the initial training period, they gave me a teller's window. The managers sat in desks on the other side of the lobby, facing the tellers so they could see everything that happened. I noticed they were especially watching me, the new girl. I went out of my way to be friendly to everyone, not only the customers, but also the other tellers. And I worked quickly. I learned the job easily and was very good it. Maybe it was because of all the shuffling of money I'd had to do at the construction company in Napoli, maybe it was because I had learned the importance of great service as a waitress and brought it to my interactions at the bank. I kept the line in front of my window moving quickly and kept the customers smiling.

One day Wilma called me over to her desk. "I need to talk to you."

"Is something wrong?" I asked as I sat down across from her.

"Yes."

I was worried because I was doing everything to do a good job. "What it is?"?

"You're not being paid enough," she said. "You're doing a great job so I'm raising you pay."

I smiled proudly. Not just because it was more money and Brandon and I could use it. But more because she'd recognized the hard work I was putting into my job. This was such a huge difference from how it had been at the Waffle House.

"I'm so happy to be here," I said. "I want to have a career here."

"You're off to a good start."

"I won't let you down."

"From here, the other managers and I can see everything that happens. So all you need to do is just keep doing a good job. We'll see it and you'll be rewarded. That's how it works here."

When I got home, I told Brandon. He was thrilled for me.

"I always told you that you're smart," he said. "Now that you're in a place with other smart people, they see it and they value it. You're going to go a long way, my love. I'm so proud of you."

Next, with both of us working and money coming in, I turned my attention to finding us a home of our own.

CHAPTER 14

As we were slowly building a new life in Massachusetts, one thing remained missing for me. I felt guilty about not marrying in the Church, not having a wedding with my family and friends there. I loved being married to Brandon. And our ceremony at the chapel in California was special to me. But still, I had always wanted a large wedding in the Catholic Church with a festive Italian reception to follow. Brandon knew that I wanted this and he told me many times that once we got stable and could afford it, we would do it.

I came home late one evening from the bank and Brandon was waiting with a dinner he had made, candles on the table.

"You worked all day, too," I said. "You shouldn't do this."

"Yes, I should."

He came over to me and grasped my hands. I could tell that something was on his mind. Before I could say anything, he lowered himself to one knee.

"Luisa Cloutier," he said. "You are the love of my life. I don't ever want to spend a day without you. You have made my life magic since I met you. And you made me the happiest man in the world when you married me. Now I want to marry you the right way, in a church in Naples. Will you marry me again?"

I felt tears streaming down my cheek. I sank down to the floor beside him and kissed his lips. "My love," I whispered to him, gazing into his eyes. "The best thing I ever did in my life is marry you. I would marry you again a hundred times."

He kissed me the he smiled and said, "I think that's a yes, right?"

• • • • •

My father agreed to pay for the reception. Angela helped plan everything in Naples, since I was here. Brandon bought two tickets. In July of 1997, we went to Logan airport to fly back to Italy for the first time since I had left four years earlier. As we rode in the taxi from Hudson, I was as happy that I was going to my family again as I was about marrying Brandon the way I'd always dreamed.

We checked in, feeling like we were walking on air. I carried my wedding gown, not wanting anything from it to get lost by the baggage people. It wouldn't fit in a suitcase anyway. Brandon and I couldn't keep our eyes off of each other. Or our hands. I knew this would be wonderful. I felt even more in love with him than I had before. Also, a guilt was going to be lifted from me. God would forgive me for getting married by a Justice of the Peace and not in a church.

"Can I have you passports please?" the ticket agent said as we checked in. We gave them to her.

Brandon asked me who was going to meet us at the airport.

"My brother."

"He knows what time we're arriving and the airline?"

"Yes. Everything is all set."

"Ms. Cloutier," the ticket agent interrupted. "May I see your Green Card.?"

"Of course." I dug into my handbag, but couldn't find it. I looked up at Brandon. "Do you have it?"

"I don't have it, no."

I looked at the ticket agent. "Isn't the passport enough?"

"If you want to come back into the country, you're going to need to have it. I can't let you leave without it."

"You have to," I said. "We're going to Italy to get married. If I'm not on this flight, I'll miss the wedding. Now, you have to let us go."

"It's government regulations. It's not me."

"I have to go." I started crying. "Please."

"It's out of my hands."

I looked at Brandon, desperate.

Brandon turned to the ticket agent. "You have to let her go. This is our wedding. You have to make an exception."

I was holding my wedding gown. "Look," I said. "Please. Help us."

"I'm sorry, there's nothing I can do."

"Let me speak to a supervisor," Brandon said. He tried to calm me as the agent went off to find a supervisor. He whispered, "It's going to be all right, my love. Don't worry."

"They have to let us go. If we miss this…"

He hushed me. "We're not going to miss it. We'll talk to them."

The supervisor came over now. "I understand your predicament," she said, "but regulations are clear. We can't let you get on the flight without your green card. How far away do you live? Can you get it and get back for the flight?"

"It'll take two hours," Brandon said.

"Can someone bring it?"

"Not for at least an hour."

She looked at her watch. "You'll miss the flight by then."

"Please," I asked her. "It's my wedding. Everything is all arranged. If we missing it, they can't just do it the next day. It'll be over. Please let us go."

Brandon said, "There's got to be some way you can let us go."

"Please!" I said again, trying to stop crying but the tears kept coming.

She took our passports and gestured for us to follow her over to a different ticket counter, away from other people. "I can lose my job," she said as she began typing into the airline computer. "I need you to promise me that before you get on the plane, you'll call someone and have they FedEx the green card to you in Italy."

"Absolutely," Brandon said. "I'll do it right now."

"You're letting us go?" I asked.

She handed us boarding passes and our passports and smiled at me. "It's your wedding. How can you not go?"

"Thank you so much. Thank you, thank you, thank you."

"Congratulations," she said. "Enjoy it."

♦ ♦ ♦ ♦

As the airline announced boarding for our flight to Rome, we stood at the pay phone and dialed Brandon's mother again. The phone rang and rang and again the answering machine picked up.

"I don't know why she isn't answering," Brandon said. "We better just leave a message." He handed me the phone. "You explain where it is, okay?"

I took the phone and left her a message, telling her exactly where the card was. "My Green Card is pink," I said. "Is not green. Please don't get it confused with my Italian driver's license which is blue and pink. Thank you. I love you."

I hung up and we ran to catch the plane.

. . . . .

The wedding was everything I had always dreamed of. Having my family standing behind us in the church made it feel right. I felt bad for Brandon because his family couldn't be there, but he said he didn't mind. If his mother and grandmother and brother and sister could have afforded it, they would have been here, too. They loved her and were glad we had got married—twice now. And, he said, I was his closest family anyway, so he did have family with him.

The ceremony was in Italian. If they spoke slowly, Brandon could understand, but getting everyone to speak slowly was not always possible. Italians are emotional and excitable and even if they start out speaking slowly, before you know it momentum gets the best of them. Everyone is talking over everyone else. Understanding what's going on isn't easy.

Still, Brandon's attitude was incredible. He looked so full of joy every time he gazed into my eyes. When it came to the part of the vows, I translated what the priest was asking.

"I, Luisa, take you, Brandon, as my husband," I said. "I promise I will be faithful to you always, when there is joy and pain, when there is health and when we are sick, and I will love you and honor you, every day." I smiled at him and said, "Until forever."

I looked at the priest as he asked me if I promised that.

"*Si*," I said, and then to Brandon I said, "I do, my love."

"Si, too," Brandon said.

The reception lasted all afternoon and was the best party I had ever been to in my life. Brandon was able to laugh and joke with people who didn't speak a word of English. And he was always attending to me, making sure I was happy and had everything I wanted.

"This is your day," he told me. "I want you to enjoy every moment."

At one point, my aunt Gianna brought over a wine class, wrapped it inside a white napkin and told us to break it.

"Are you Jewish or Catholic?" Brandon asked.

"That is the custom here," I told him. "We break it and count the pieces, and that is the number of years we'll be happily married."

"Really? Give me that." He grabbed the glass. "By the time I'm done with it, it'll be broken into a thousand pieces."

We laughed and drank and that night made love in a beautiful hotel by the sea. The honeymoon was short because we both had to get back to work. We could only stay in Italy for two weeks.

While we were dealing with the wedding, I tried not to think about going back to America, but once everything was finished, I began to be nervous because nothing had arrived by FedEx, and without my Green Card, I couldn't go back.

Brandon called his mother because time was running out.

"Yes, I sent it," she said. "As soon as I got the message. But I didn't listen to the messages until two days ago. But it's on its way. I should arrive any day."

"Italy is not like America," I told Brandon. "Things don't go on time like there."

"It'll arrive," he told me. "Everything will be all right."

The day before we were scheduled to leave, the FedEx driver stopped at my sister's house where we were staying. I ran down the stairs to meet him, and he handed me the envelope from the U.S.

"*Tanta grazie,*" I told him.

I loved Italy, and I loved being with my family again, but I knew my future wasn't there, my life wasn't there. We were building a life in Hudson and we needed to get back.

I tore open the flap, reached in and pulled out my Italian driver's license.

My friend Mario picked us up to drive us to the airport in Rome. He worked for the Carbinieri, Italy's national police, and drove as if the speeding laws didn't apply to him. I was nervous most of the ride, thinking we were going to crash. Accidents were more common in Italy than in the U.S. and the outcomes were usually more severe. Brandon didn't seem worried about that, but he looked lost in thought, concerned about the Green Card issue.

When we got to the airport and tried to check in for the flight, the customs agent looked at my passport and asked for my Green Card. I explained what had happened, showed him the Italian driver's license and assured him that Brandon's mother would be waiting at the airport with the Green Card when we arrived.

He handed the passport back to me. "I'm sorry. You cannot leave the country."

"What do you mean? I have to go."

"I can't help you. Without the Green Card, you can't go."

"But I have to. We have to get back to work. I'll lose my job. No, we have to go."

The customs agent pointed at Brandon. "He can go. You have to stay."

"I'm not leaving without my wife," Brandon said.

The customs agent shrugged. "There's nothing I can do."

We realized he wasn't going to give in like the airline agent in Boston had. He wasn't concerned about our problem.

"My mother can send the Green Card today," Brandon told me. "We'll get it in a couple days."

"We'll lose the tickets. We can't afford two new tickets. One, maybe."

"I'm not going to leave you here."

"This is my country," I said. "I have my family here. Mario will take me back to Angela's. I'll be okay. You go home. When the Green Card comes, I'll buy a new ticket and follow. It will be okay."

"Are you sure?"

"I'll miss you every moment."

"So will I," Brandon said.

I kissed him, a long kiss to make sure he remembered me. We hadn't been apart overnight since he had left the Marines, and the thought of it did make me sad, and a little nervous, but I knew it was the right thing to do. We had to be as strong as our love for each other and endure the short separation.

"Call me when you arrive," I told him. "I'll be waiting."

* * * * *

My Green Card did come, but leaving was not easy. As is the custom in Italy, things don't go smoothly. We returned to Rome a few days later and went to the American Consulate because they had to verify my information and sign release papers allowing me to return home. I was eager to straighten this out so Angela and I went early, when the doors opened.

The computers were not working when we arrived there, so we had to wait. Then it was lunch and no one was working, so we had to come back later. Then it was late in the afternoon and they were closing soon so we had to come back the next day. The next day, it started all over again. The computers were down, there wasn't enough time, someone wasn't at their desk.

By the third day, I was fed up with the Italian way of doing things. After four years in the U.S., I was used to the efficiency and didn't have the patience for doing everything slowly and not being helpful. Finally I had reached my limit.

"Listen to me," I told the man at the consulate. "I have to go. I have a job waiting for me. My husband is waiting for me. I've been here three days. I need to go."

"We have to verify the information and the computers are down."

"I don't care if the computers are down." I reached down and picked up his telephone. "Call and verify whatever you need to verify," I said. "But let me go home."

"Calm down, signora. Let me see what I can do. Have a seat."

I reluctantly sat. Fifteen minutes later he came back.

"We verified everything," he said. "Show me your airline ticket and I can release you to go back."

"My ticket expired a week ago."

"I can't release you without a ticket."

Angela and her boyfriend Luca were with me. "I'll buy you one now," Luca said. "You pay me back later."

The consulate man looked at his watch. "We close in an hour. You better hurry."

We ran to the travel agency a block away and pushed the woman there to quickly get us a ticket for a plane leaving later that night. Then we ran back to the Consulate and arrived just as they were about to lock the door. I knew they were going to try to tell us to come back tomorrow, but I glared at the man at the door before he could say anything. He let us in and within a few minutes they finally released me to return home.

As I waited in the airport that evening for my flight to depart, I realized that I needed to get my U.S. Citizenship so I would never have to deal with this situation again.

Less than two years later, at Faneuil Hall in Boston, I was sworn in as a U.S. Citizen.

CHAPTER 15

Our lives steadily improved financially. Brandon got a better job at PC Connection as a sales rep, with more money and better hours. He also decided to pursue his lifelong interest in fitness and got certified as a personal trainer. I was promoted a few times at the bank and then I accepted an offer for even more money working for Hewlett Packard. We saved up enough to put a down payment on a house and we became homeowners.

Both of us were busy most of the time and had less time to spend with each other. And while we were successful in our jobs, neither of us was happy. I hated my work at Hewlett Packard to the point that it made me sick to go there every day. Brandon kept saying that the sales rep job at PC Connection was not his future, but for now it was secure money, as was my job.

Then Brandon learned that his company would be laying off people soon. Instead of panicking, he saw it as an opportunity. He had always wanted to make fitness his career, and this seemed like the time to make the leap. With his personal trainer certification in hand, Brandon applied for work at Global Fitness. The manager liked him and gave him a chance. A chance was all Brandon ever needed.

It did not take long before he showed the manager how valuable he was as a trainer. The customers liked him right away. He was handsome and had an infectious personality. He made people want to work out. Everyone wanted to train with him. He generated new membership packages and renewals like the manager had never seen before. Clients were inviting him to parties. He started making more money. He loved it.

And I loved seeing him happy and successful.

My work, though, continued being misery for me. I knew we needed the money, and I still wanted a career, so I went every day, but Brandon could see every night how unhappy I was.

One evening, after a long tiring day for both of us, while we were sitting on the back deck of our house looking at the stars and sipping wine, Brandon hugged me and said, "My love, I'm working on getting you out of your job."

"What do you mean?"

"I'm going to open a business."

"What kind of business?"

"Personal training."

"Do you think that can be a business?"

"I know it can. More people come to that gym for me than for everyone else combined," he said. "because I give my clients results. People will pay for that. Right now I'm working my butt off to make somebody else rich. I'm going to open my own place, and then all the work I do will be to make us rich."

"I believe you can," I said.

"I know I can. And I promise you that I will give you a good life. After I open my business, you'll never have to work for anyone else, ever again."

"I love you," I said, feeling safe in his arms, his words echoing in my head. He made me believe. He had a magical way of relaxing me, of making me feel better no matter what was happening. He could make me forget anything and have hope.

I felt guilty that I made him feel sad for me and I told myself that I had to be stronger for him, the way he was strong for me. We were a team, and together we could get through anything, do anything, forever.

We needed money to open a business, so we had to keep working, saving as much as we could. Brandon worked extra hours at the gym. The more he worked, the more people he trained, and that meant the more money he could earn. He came home exhausted most nights. I hardly ever saw him. Feeling lonely, I thought a lot about my family in Italy and missed seeing them.

I got a new job as Assistant Manager at DCU, another bank. I had more responsibility, more money, more stress. I worked later, too. Why rush home to an empty house, I thought. I started getting more attention from men at work than from Brandon, and that made me angry. I wanted the attention to come from him, but it never did. It seemed all he cared about was his work, making his dream come true. I felt like I had nothing, like I didn't matter.

This continued for months. We withdrew from each other, became more distant. I found myself spending my time at home emailing other people rather than talking with him. It was as if we were living two different lives. We never made love anymore. I wasn't sure we even loved each other any longer.

The first weekend that Brandon didn't come home was like a knife to my heart. He said he'd spent it at a friend's house, but in my heart I knew he was with another woman. I pretended like I didn't care and barely talked to him that week. A few weeks later he did it again, stayed away for the entire weekend, claiming that he was with a male friend and networking with potential clients that would be good for his business when he opened it.

I started going out for drinks with coworkers. Men would hit on me all the time, but I would always resist them. I was still married to Brandon, and my vows meant something to me. This went on for months and months. I felt our marriage rotting around me and it was torture. I wanted it to be different, but I didn't know how to fix it.

Brandon noticed that I was communicating with people on the computer and he asked me what was going on.

"Nothing," I said.

"Don't tell me nothing. What are you doing?"

"You're asking me that? Ask yourself."

"What's that supposed to mean?"

"Just leave me alone, okay? I need some space."

"Talk to me, Luisa."

But I wouldn't. I found silence much more tolerable. I was falling apart and I did not want to let that out into the open by talking about it. I couldn't handle that.

But the more I isolated myself from him, the farther away he drifted and the lonelier I felt. I was sinking deeper and deeper into a black hole and I didn't see the way out. My life had become nothing but pain.

One morning I was sitting on our bed and I just started to cry. Brandon came in and saw me. He hurried over.

"What's wrong, my love?" he said.

I shook my head, unable to answer.

"Talk to me. What's wrong?"

I took a breath and stopped my weeping. "I don't want this anymore," I whispered.

"What do you mean?"

"I have to say it!" I hesitated and calmed myself. "I want out. Go find yourself another woman, someone who will make you happy. It isn't me."

Brandon kneeled in front of me. "Luisa, don't say that." He grasped both my hands and made me look into his eyes. "You know I love you, and I know you love me too."

I said nothing. Tears streamed from my eyes. I had to look at the floor to try to control my pain.

He said, "My love, it hurts me to see you cry."

I still could not say anything.

"Look into my eyes," he said. He gently lifted my chin so I was looking at him. "Remember when we fell in love?"

Thinking of those days, I began to weep harder.

"I know you still feel the same way," he said.

The only answer I could give him was to shake my head, no.

° ° ° °

I continued to push him away for months, and the more I did this, the deeper I sank into depression. I felt lost. When I got so low that all I could see was the pit of who I was, the depths of my heart and soul, I saw that the only thing that really mattered to me in life was the love Brandon and I had found years ago and had built piece by piece into the most solid thing in my life. I needed that love. I needed Brandon. I needed to stop pushing him away, stop letting life get between us, and make our marriage the priority.

I went to him and tried to show my affection, but it was too late. I kept trying, though. Then one night, when his mother was coming over for dinner and we were getting dressed upstairs, I came up behind him and kissed his neck.

He pulled away then said, "We need to talk."

I could see by the look on his face that this was serious and it scared me. I said, "Yes."

We sat down on the bed and for a moment stared at each other in silence. Brandon gazed off, looking troubled, struggling to find the words. Finally he turned back to me and looked directly into my eyes.

"I don't know how to say this other than just saying it," he said.

"Say what?"

"I have feelings for someone else."

His words hit me like stones, each impact burning with pain. I steeled myself, trying not to show it.

"Before I do anything," he said, "I want to ask you for a divorce."

I couldn't hold it in any longer and started to cry.

He stared at me, looking shocked. "Why are you crying?" he said. "I thought that's what you wanted."

"No," I said. "I know it's my fault. But I love you."

"I love you too, Luisa," Brandon said, and for an instant I felt hopeful, but then he shook his head and said, "But I'm not *in love* with you anymore."

Tears streamed out of his eyes too.

I shook my head. I didn't want to believe him.

"I'm sorry, Luisa," he said.

CHAPTER 16

I told Brandon to move out. He'd started seeing another woman, someone he'd met at work. A friend of ours told me that it wasn't Brandon who initiated it, that the woman had pursued him. He must have liked the attention she gave him, that I hadn't been giving him.

I had no interest in seeing anyone else. I was just trying to make it through each day. I stopped eating and lost a lot of weight. I lost interest in everything.

One day I received a FedEx package. It reminded me of the Green Card fiasco in Italy and that made me think about how much love Brandon and I had had and how that was now gone. I wanted it back. I wanted him back. I opened the envelope to find divorce papers from Brandon, with a note that I needed to sign them. I had no intention of signing anything. Instead I ripped up the papers and threw them away.

I kept in touch with Brandon's mother, Lora. We had been through a lot together, and while she loved her son, she also had come to love me. She called a lot to find out how I was. I could cry with her like I could with no one else. She felt bad about what was happening.

"You should go out on a date with someone," she told me. "He is. You should, too. You'll feel better."

I knew that wouldn't make me feel better.

I stayed by myself, hating every minute that I was alone in our house. Sometimes I even felt scared. Old New England houses make weird noises, and when you're a woman alone in the middle of the night, your imagination easily gets away from you.

One night the noises scared me so much that I had to get out. I fled to the only person I knew would take me in. Brandon's mother. Lora let me come in and told me I could sleep there as long as I wanted. She made some tea and she and I sat in the kitchen, talking.

"I wonder where Brandon is," I said. I knew he was with some woman, but I didn't know who or where and that bothered me. I still loved him. It hurt not knowing.

"Do you really want to know?" she asked me.

"Yes. We were together so long, it's hard to just have him gone and not know where he is, what he's doing."

"You *really* want to know?"

"Yes. Why? Do you know?"

"I know."

I leaned closer. "Where is he? How do you know anyway?"

"Gabriela," Lora said, "the woman I used to work with, she saw him. She told me where he's staying."

"Where?"

"In the house across the street from her. One day she was looking out the window and recognized him moving in with the neighbor. He's been there ever since."

"Really? Whose house it is? Who is he staying with?"

"I don't know her name."

"Where is it?"

"Why?" Lora said.

"I want to go there. Just to see her."

"You can't do that."

"Why not?"

Lora didn't have an answer.

"Please," I said. "I really have to do this."

Lora thought for moment then she let out a sigh. "Well, you can't go now, in the middle of the night. And you can't go alone. I'll take you there in the morning. But just to see. Not to do anything, right?"

"Of course," I said.

· · · · ·

In the morning, before leaving, I made sure I was dressed well and my hair and makeup were done. I wanted to look good in case Brandon saw me, or that woman saw me. I didn't want her or Brandon to think he was better than me.

When we pulled up in front of the house in Lora' car, Brandon's car was parked in the driveway. I got out of the car.

"Where are you going?" Lora asked.

"I'll be right back. Wait here."

I walked past the front lawn and up to the door. I didn't see a name on the mailbox. I wondered who she was. I wanted to see her. And to talk to Brandon. I wasn't sure exactly what I was going to say to him, but I couldn't just leave as though this were all right. I rang the doorbell.

As I waited, I looked at the windows, the yard, Brandon's car, the door again, back at the windows. A dog barked inside. I knew someone was in there. I pressed the bell again. No one answered. I looked over at Brandon's car again. He was here. When I turned back, I saw the curtain on one of the windows move and was sure I'd seen a small figure move behind it. *Her.* I rang the bell again but still no one answered.

I was getting more and more angry as I waited and no one opened. I imagined what would happen if she opened the door. Before she could get a word out, I'd grab her by the hair and teach her to sleep with another woman's husband.

I took a step back and peered up at the second floor of the house. That's probably where the bedroom would be.

"Brandon!" I called out. "Come outside. I just want to talk with you."

I waited, but he did not show himself, no answer.

"I'm not leaving until you come out," I shouted up toward the windows. "I can wait here all day."

I waited. Still no response from inside. From either of them.

I walked back to the front door and pressed the bell. Then I knocked. The dog barked again. But what were the cowards doing inside, I wondered.

"Brandon!" I shouted again.

I walked around to the side of the house where his car was parked and shouted to him again, but he wasn't budging. I could be as stubborn. I went back to the front to sit on the stairs and wait until they came out, but as I was about to sit down a police car, lights flashing, pulled up into the driveway.

I felt exasperated that now I had to deal with this cop. The officer was a man in his fifties, with a stomach like a pregnant woman's. Every few steps, he had to stop to pull up his pants along with his belt, holster and pistol. He stood in front of me, hands on his hips, and told me I had to leave.

"My husband is inside this house," I said, putting my hands on my hips. "I want to talk to him."

"Ma'am, this is private property. They don't want you here so you need to leave the property."

"Not until my husband comes out."

"It's not going to happen that way. You have to leave."

"I want to talk to my husband."

"He doesn't want to talk to you."

"Is that so?" I said.

"That's so. Now I'm trying to be nice. You have to leave or I'll arrest you. One way or the other, you're leaving here. Do you understand me?"

"I have the right to talk to my husband?"

"Not here you don't. Now let's go," he said, reaching for my arm.

I pulled my arm away. "All right, I'll leave."

His expression turned harder now. He didn't like that I pulled my arm away, but I didn't need him escorting me off. I started walking toward Lora's car. Lora was standing outside the car, watching, looking worried.

The policeman followed me.

"Do me a favor," I said to him. I spoke loud, so they'd here me inside. "If you see my husband, tell him that he doesn't have the balls to come out and talk to me." I twisted my head and shouted toward the house, "Do you hear me?"

· · · · ·

Several men had asked me out since Brandon and I had separated. I always said no. But now, after seeing Brandon's car outside that woman's house, I accepted the invitation from Manny, the cousin of a friend of ours, someone both Brandon and I knew socially. At parties, Manny always looked at me in ways that Brandon didn't like. I had never had an interest in him, but when he called me, I think I agreed more as revenge against Brandon than as something I looked forward to doing.

I wrote down his name, the address of the restaurant in Boston where he wanted to take me, and the day and time, and stuck it to the refrigerator. When the weekend finally came, I dreaded going on the date, but I went through with it. Lora encouraged me to go. A few friends told me it would be good for me. I didn't look at it as a date. I was just having dinner with someone.

And that's all it turned out to be. We ate, we talked about my marriage and his longtime relationship that had just broken up. We both had broken hearts. We got along well, but there was no chemistry between us, no attraction. When it ended, we hugged and that was it. It was a pleasant night with a friend.

When I got home, I saw that Brandon had come by and left a check on the kitchen counter. He still had a key and always paid the mortgage and the utility bills. I also noticed that the note with Manny's information on it that I had stuck to the refrigerator was now on the counter, near the check. Brandon had seen it.

The next morning the phone rang early. It was Brandon.

"Did you find the check I left last night?" he said.

"Yes. Thank you."

"No problem. Um, did you go out?"

"Yes."

He was silent for a moment. "With who?"

"Paula's cousin, Manny. Remember him?"

"Yeah." He was silent for a moment then he cleared his throat and said, "How did it go?"

"It wasn't a date, Brandon," I told him. "There's no attraction."

"No, no, I didn't think that. I was just...just asking."

"You should have come to the door," I said.

He knew what I meant. "It wasn't me who called the police. It was her. I tried to stop her."

"It's a good thing she didn't open the door. For her sake."

He let out a nervous laugh. "I think so. We're not together anymore."

"Why not?"

"She meant nothing. It was just...you know. She never meant anything to me."

· · · · ·

He started calling me more often, asking how I was doing. My friend Pat said that he had no right to check up on me. I said I didn't mind. I liked talking to him. I loved him. I was the one who pushed him away, not the other way around. Pat kept saying that I shouldn't put up with him, that he was the one who cheated. But I knew there was much more to it than that.

Then one day the call was different. Instead of just asking how I was doing, he said, "Luisa, I want you to have dinner with me."

His words took my breath away. I was confused, but I agreed.

When we were together in the restaurant, I looked across the table at him and asked, "Why did you want to have dinner with me?"

"I missed you."

"Now? After all this time?"

"No, not just now. I've missed you for a long, long time," he said. He reached over and grasped my hands. "Luisa, I missed you even before we started living apart. It just took us being apart for me to realize how much I missed you, and how important you are to me."

"Is that why you sent me divorce papers?"

"I thought that's what you wanted."

"You keep using that excuse. What is it that you want?"

"The same thing I always wanted. You, by my side. What do you want?" he asked.

I thought a moment, took a breath to calm myself and said, "The same thing."

. . . . .

Two weeks before Christmas, Brandon told me, "Luisa, I want to come home. I want to be with you forever."

"I do too," I said.

The day he walked back into the house, it became a home again. We were so happy to be together that neither of us questioned the other, neither of us had any jealousy or doubts. We were meant to be together and never be apart again.

CHAPTER 17

The next summer Brandon and I flew to Santa Barbara, California, to attend a conference on starting your own personal training business. After three days there, Brandon was sure he could do it.

We walked along the beach the last night before we left. The place was so beautiful. We both felt energized.

"We'll have to give up a lot of things," Brandon told me, "in order to do this. It's going to take a lot of money to get off the ground, but I know we can do it."

"Where do we get the money?" I asked.

"I'll figure that part out. But I think this is our time. We have to take this chance."

"I believe in you, Brandon. If you say you can do it, I'll take the risk."

"I can do it. I promise."

I held me, and I felt safe and happy and confident.

"Maybe someday we can retire here," I said as we continued to walk. "It's so beautiful."

"As long as I'm with you, anywhere is beautiful."

· · · · ·

Every week we would meet to discuss the business plan. Brandon worked out more and more of the details as time went on. He found a franchise that he said would be good for us to buy into. And he figured out where we would get the money.

"We'll sell the house," he said. "The market has gone up a lot since we bought it three years ago. We can make over a hundred thousand dollars profit and with the money saved in the bank, that's how we'll pay for the business."

"Where will we live?"

"We'll get a smaller place. I know it's going backward a little, but remember I said we would have to give up some things? This is one. But it'll only be for a short time. Once the business takes off, I'll buy you the house of your dreams."

· · · · ·

The realtor told Brandon that the price he wanted was too high. The market had gone up, but not *that* much. No one was going to pay that.

"That's my price," Brandon told him. "Sell it at that price or I'll find another realtor."

Less than a month later the realtor called to say he had an offer, at the price Brandon wanted.

· · · · ·

Three months later, we opened our Fitness Together studio.

Brandon had such a good reputation in the area that people came to us right away. We started doing excellent business. I wanted to be by Brandon's side so I quit my job, got certified myself, and began working as a trainer. I loved it. Not only because I was near Brandon, but also because the work itself was satisfying.

Instead of numbers and contracts and financial matters, I was helping individual people improve their lives. It truly was *personal* training. I developed close friendships with my clients as I helped them modify their bodies, improve their health and make their life better. With many I became like family. I worked the way Brandon had taught me, with a positive attitude and treating each person as though when I was training them, nothing else in the world mattered. I wasn't talking with another trainer or another customer. I was as focused with my client at that moment as much as they were. And I got results. That was Brandon's method. And it worked.

Our business became successful quickly. Within a few months we became one of the top grossing franchises in the company. It felt good to have the stresses of money gone, but to be able to do that while spending all day, every day, with the man of my dreams was more than I had ever hoped for.

Brandon found us a new home, as beautiful as he had promised. Much larger than the two of us needed, but Brandon said he wanted me to have the best. We'd both worked hard, sacrificed a lot. We deserved this house. To me it was a mansion, with two master bedrooms, plenty of guestrooms for both our families, a kitchen fit for a chef, more than three thousand square feet to make our new life together. I felt like a princess who had everything she ever wanted, and more.

We were careful this time not to make the same mistake as before, not to let our work take over our lives and push us apart. We made time for each other. We were determined to keep our marriage strong. We dated. We paid attention to each other.

We even managed to take a week off for Valentine's Day and go to Jamaica. Getting away from the business was difficult, but we made it happen, and it turned out to be the most romantic week I had ever spent in my life. We laughed and danced and played on the beach, and we made love under the stars at night. We left the island feeling even closer than we'd ever felt before.

On the flight home Brandon said, "We should get married again."

"You want to marry me again? You were crazy twice already."

"Then let's be crazy three times."

"Are you sure?"

"I've never been more sure of anything in my life."

Looking into his eyes, I saw the love he had for me. All we had been through hadn't dimmed it one bit. Nor had it lessened my love for him.

"You're not sure?" he asked.

"I'm sure."

"Then let's do it. We'll get married in Jamaica. On the beach. This time both families will be there. It'll be the best one of all. Until the fourth time..."

Life was beautiful. Even my dreams hadn't been this good. I thanked God for our happiness and I committed never to let it slip away from us again. Experience made us live wiser. Having been through that pain would now assure us a time of joy.

PART FOUR

CHAPTER 18

SUMMER 2013
Boylston, Massachusetts

I awoke in the middle of the night, terrified that my father was going to die.

Not having seen him in years, I couldn't be sure about his health. I talked to Angela on the phone often, and she would have told me if he wasn't doing well. If she knew. But sometimes you can't tell.

I lay in bed, staring up at the ceiling, the vague image of a man clutching his heart swimming in my head. As if he were having a heart attack. Or maybe the dream was telling me that my father's heart was broken from not seeing me in such a long time. I had been away from Italy too long. I needed to go back. My father was getting older. I needed to pay attention to the premonition.

I didn't sleep any more that night. I sat up, awake, thinking about my father and listening to Brandon breathing beside me. I got strength from his proximity. I thought about waking him up, but decided to let him sleep. He had been exhausted when he went to bed, as he was most nights. Besides, what could he do? He would say it's only a dream, everything is going to be all right.

As well as he knew me, and as much as he loved me, he couldn't truly understand the things that were normal and unquestioned to me, to the culture I came from. Dreams and premonitions were things we listened to. We prayed to a God that no one saw, and believed that it meant something. Premonitions were just as real.

I looked at the red digits of the glowing clock beside the bed. 3:22. In

Italy it was six hours later, 9:22, so my father had been up for a couple hours. Thinking it might calm my nerves a bit, I went downstairs to the kitchen and tried to call him. He didn't answer at his apartment. I tried his cell phone. No answer there either. Instead of putting me at ease, the calls only made me worry more.

Brandon woke up at 5:00 to get to the gym for his early appointments. When he came downstairs, I told him about the feeling I had and said, "I need to go visit him."

"Definitely. If you want to go, I'll make it happen. If I could get away, I would go with you, but I need to stay and run the business."

Going to Jamaica and leaving the business closed had been problematic enough. Brandon said we couldn't do that again yet. There was too much going on. We had begun grooming one of the trainers we'd hired to be able to take some management responsibilities. Some day he would know enough to step in and take care of things while we went away, but he wasn't there yet. So one of us had to stay.

"I really think I need to go," I said.

"I agree. Call him, work things out, we'll make the reservation."

"I called him. I can't reach him."

He tried to call with me a few more times before he had to leave for work. Finally my father answered his cell phone. He said he was doing all right. I didn't tell him about my premonition. I called Angela next, and she said there was nothing wrong with him, but she agreed that he was getting older and that I should come to visit. Bit by bit, my fear subsided. From what he and Angela were saying, he wasn't in immediate danger. I felt relieved. I made plans to visit in a couple months and jumped back into my work.

· · · · ·

Brandon and I worked hard on building the business and on keeping our relationship solid and loving. We made it a point to go out to dinner often. It wasn't the healthiest way to eat, and we were living as healthy a lifestyle as possible, since that's what we were advocating to our clients and that was what we both believed in. But breaking the meal plan we usually had was worth it if it meant Brandon and I would remain close and in love.

Brandon was too generous with me, continuously buying me gifts that I didn't ask for or even need. When I objected to his giving me more and more, he would always say that he did it because he wanted to give to me. It made him feel good. And I deserved it.

"You're crazy," I'd always say.

He'd always laugh and say, "Crazy in love with you."

One night, as we were about to go out to dinner, he told me to hang on a second. He took out a jewelry box and handed it to me.

"What's this?" I asked.

"Open it."

"What is it?"

"Open it," he insisted.

"Why do you keep buying me gifts? I don't need anything. I have everything."

"It makes me happy to do it," he said. "Please. Open it, okay?"

I opened the box and was shocked to see the shimmering diamond bracelet. "Oh, my God, this is beautiful. But it must have cost a fortune?"

"Put it on."

He took it out of the box. I watched his large, strong hands gently put it on my wrist.

"You like it?" he said.

"It's incredible."

"It's ten carats!"

I was stunned. "You're crazy!"

"Crazy for you."

"No, really, Brandon. This is too much. I can't take this." I started to take it off. "It's too expensive."

He put his hand over mine and stopped me. "My love, compared to how much you're worth to me, the bracelet cost nothing."

"I don't need this," I said.

"I need to give it to you. You like it, right?"

"Yes. It's beautiful."

"Never take it off, okay?"

"Brandon…"

"Promise me. I want you to have it and wear it always, and know that it is because I love you and because I'm so thankful for everything you've done for me."

"Everything *I've* done?"

"Yes. You put up with a lot, for many years. And you worked hard, for the business, for our marriage, for me."

"I do only what any wife would do."

"No, my love. You're something special."

"So are you, Brandon."

I grabbed his face and kissed him. He surrounded me in his strong arms, pulling me into his world of safety and love. I had made mistakes in my life, who hasn't? But marrying Brandon, leaving home to follow him, was the most right thing I had ever done.

I took a breath and said, "But please don't keep spending so much money on me. Please."

"This is the last thing," he said. "I promise."

He smiled at me, that loving smile of his, and I knew that this wouldn't be the last thing. It was a promise he couldn't keep.

I shook my head and laughed. "*Bugiardo*," I said, calling him a liar in Italian.

"What does that mean?"

"It means I'm so lucky to have you."

"*Bugiardo*, me too," he said.

CHAPTER 19

Coming from the temperate climate of Naples, Italy, I found the winters in Massachusetts were most difficult for me. Brandon did well with the snow and wind and freezing temperatures, but I struggled and was happy to stay inside as much as possible. I did a lot of the computer work for our business, keeping the books, maintaining contact with clients and vendors. Brandon was happy to leave all that to me.

On a morning in January, 2014, after having breakfast with Brandon, I was on the computer, the phone lodged between my shoulder and ear, and I was talking to Norton antivirus customer service department, trying to sort out an issue with our PC.

Brandon came up behind me, put his hand on my shoulder and kissed my neck. "I'm going to take a shower," he whispered to me.

I squeezed his hand then turned to face him. I covered the mouthpiece of the phone and told Brandon, "I'll be up as soon as I finish this and clean the kitchen."

"Leave the kitchen," he said. "We'll do it later." He looked beat. I'd never seen him so serious. And he had a funny look on his face, but I didn't understand what it was.

"Everything okay?" I asked.

He nodded.

"Go on up. I'll come soon," I said.

He headed upstairs. I resumed my conversation with the Norton Antivirus people. The woman on the other end of the line was telling me things to do, hit this key, click on that, scroll to the bottom of the page and hit OK. Meanwhile I could hear Brandon turn on the shower upstairs. I needed to find a way to do more for him. He was always doing for me, giving to me, worrying about me. He said I did a lot for him, made his live worth living, but I didn't feel like I did enough. I was determined to change that.

Straightening out the antivirus software took another fifteen minutes. When I hung up, I went into the kitchen to straighten up. I had no intention to leave it for Brandon to do. I worked for another ten minutes and was almost finished when I heard it. It made me stop what I was doing and just listen to make sure I really was hearing it.

I stood motionless and alone, not making a sound, just listening.

There it was. The faint hissing of the shower upstairs. Brandon was still showering. I glanced at the clock on the microwave. How much time had passed since he went upstairs? I'd resolved the matter with Norton and nearly cleaned the kitchen. It was close to a half hour. And he was still showering. I knew he liked to take long showers, but even for him this seemed longer than usual.

I went back to cleaning, hurrying to finish. The hiss of the shower continued, gnawing at my conscience. I started to think that something wasn't right.

Leaving the kitchen unfinished, I went through the living room toward the stairs. I peered up at the hallway upstairs. The sound of the shower was louder here for some reason, as if asking me to hurry.

I headed up the stairs, at first just with quick steps, but then leaping to the top. Upstairs, the sound was even louder. It felt almost as though it was yelling at me.

I rushed up the hallway to the master bedroom, blew through the door and started to turn toward the bathroom door. Brandon was right there. On the bathroom floor, his body twisted in a surreal position, the shower running beside him, screeching and spitting steam.

"Brandon!" I screamed and ran to him.

The bathroom was like a steam room, the air so thick and heavy I could barely breathe. I dropped to my knees beside Brandon and began to shake him.

"Brandon! Oh, God, what's wrong?"

His eyes remained closed, even when I shook him again.

"Hold on, Brandon! Hold on, my love!"

I knew how to do CPR because it was part of the personal trainer certification. I started to do chest compressions on him, but I realized I needed to call for an ambulance. I grabbed the cell phone from the pocket of my jeans. My hands trembling, I punched 9-1-1. As I waited for it to connect, I said out loud, "Please, God, don't take him from me. Please. Please."

The dispatcher came on instantly.

"What is your emergency?"

"Help! Hurry! My husband needs an ambulance!"

"Okay, slow down, ma'am. Can you tell me what's happening?"

"My husband needs an ambulance. He's on the floor. He's not breathing. He needs help! Hurry."

The woman kept telling me to calm down and kept asking me stupid questions. I just wanted her to get off the phone so she could tell the ambulance to come.

"Please send an ambulance!"

"They're already on their way. Do you know how to do CPR?" She wanted me to start doing it again.

As I pressed on his chest, I looked up toward the ceiling and yelled, "Please, God!" Tears streamed from my eyes. "Please don't take him away from me!"

I stared down at Brandon. His face was moving from my thrusts on his chest, but he wasn't waking up.

"Don't leave me!" I screamed at him. "Come back! Please come back!

CHAPTER 20

Angela and Rodolfo flew in from Italy the next day. Brandon's mother Lora flew up from Florida. They took care of the funeral plans.

I was a wreck. For days I couldn't sleep. I didn't want to eat but they all kept pushing me. The only strength I had came from being inside the house, *his* house. I treasured it as though it were Brandon. Everything I looked at I saw him, everything I touched I felt connected to him. This house meant so much to him. As did the business. And he left them to me. I wasn't clear about much those days, but I was very clear that my mission was to preserve our home and our studio.

Two days before the funeral, I got dressed and went downstairs. Angela had made breakfast, but I declined.

"You have to eat, Luisa."

I turned to my younger brother, who was spooning sugar into his espresso. "Rodolfo, can you drive me to the studio?"

He looked surprised by the question. He glanced at Angela.

Angela said, "Why?"

"I have some appointments with new clients that were scheduled a long time ago. I have to go. We can't lose them."

"You can call and reschedule."

"No. I have to go."

"Luisa, this is foolish. Change them for another day. Or let someone else go."

I shook my head.

"You have employees. They can meet the clients."

"I have to do it."

"I'll go down there," Rodolfo said, "and I'll ask the people who work for you to take care of it. Don't worry about it, Luisa."

"If you don't take me I'm going to drive myself," I said. "I have to do this."

They realized there was no point in arguing with me.

· · · · ·

When Rodolfo and I arrived at the studio, Garren stared at me, stunned that I was there. He glanced at Rodolfo, as though to ask him why I was there.

"Garren," I said. "Please do me a favor."

"Sure, Luisa. Anything."

Garren was the trainer who had been with us the longest, since shortly after we had opened the studio. Brandon had hired him and had given him more and more responsibility over time. Garren couldn't run the business, but he was the person we left in charge whenever we had to be away for a few days.

He had just opened the studio for the morning, but there were no clients there. Most of the employees hadn't arrived yet either.

"I want to have a meeting with everyone when they come in," I told him. "Can you set it up, maybe in an hour?"

"Of course. Sure." Garren glanced again at Rodolfo, as though he were waiting for my brother to step in and say something. Rodolfo remained silent. Garren turned back to me.

"You don't need to be here today, Luisa," he said. "I mean, I can take care of things if you want to…"

"Thank you, but if you could just set up the meeting…"

"Yeah, sure, no problem."

I went to my office in the back of the studio and closed the door before Rodolfo could follow me inside. For most the next hour, with the door closed, I cried.

· · · · ·

When I sat down in the reception area with my trainer, my eyes were dry and clear, though a bit swollen. I wasn't sure how obvious it was that I had been crying. In front of them I kept all of my emotions inside. Though I'd known some of them for years, I had always been private when it came to my personal life. That wasn't going to change now.

No one said a word. I saw a few wet eyes staring back at me. I got right to the point.

"I want all of you to know that nothing is going to change here," I said. "The studio isn't going to close. No one is losing your job. I will take care of everything."

They continued staring in silence. I saw some of the heads nod. My head wasn't completely clear. Not everything registered. What was clear was the pain in my heart. It hurt physically, as if I'd just sprinted an entire 10K.

I took a deep breath and steeled myself so I could continue.

"The show goes on," I said. "We need to make Brandon proud of us, so let's wipe our tears and do whatever it takes to be successful. For Brandon. Okay?"

They all said okay.

I went back to my office before anyone could come up and tell me how bad they felt for me or try to hug me. They meant well, but it wasn't comforting. None of that helped. If they wanted to do something good, they could bring Brandon back, but since none of them could do that, since *nobody* could do that, I preferred they said nothing at all.

That day and the days that followed, when I wasn't with a new client I stayed in my office, reminding myself to be strong, to put on the mask for everyone else. I felt completely lost. I think I went to work because that was the only thing I knew how to do on autopilot. I didn't have to think about what to do. It came naturally by now. That's what I needed.

Losing my mother two decades earlier had been the most traumatic thing in my life. But now, losing Brandon was so much worse. The pain was so deep it afflicted every part of my body, every part of who I was.

· · · · ·

The one day my mask came off was the day of Brandon's funeral. He hadn't been Catholic, but he had gone to church with me many times. He'd come to come to love the religion, and especially Father Walsh, the pastor of the church we sometimes went to. We held the funeral there.

It was January and snowing heavily. Clouds darkened the sky. The air was so cold that it was difficult to breathe. I wore a heavy black coat, hoping I could hide inside it, hide from what had to be done that day. Much of the funeral was a blur to me. I didn't see the people around me. I didn't see Father Walsh.

I tried not to see the coffin in front of the altar, but that was the one thing that remained clear in my head throughout. A constant reminder that Brandon was dead. Brandon was inside and no longer with me. No longer would I feel his arms around me, no longer hear his voice saying "my love." If only I could open the casket and take him out, bring him back to life. Maybe if I'd done CPR better, sooner. Maybe if I did it now. Maybe if I'd been a better person. There had to be something I could do to still have him beside me.

I had no idea how to face the world without him, and once this funeral was over, I would be without him forever. It was a reality I could not bear.

Rodolfo stood beside me during the funeral mass. A couple times I felt like I was going to faint, but he held me up, just as he had done in the house before we'd left for the church. When it came time for the eulogy, my legs didn't want to move. It took all my strength to get up from the pew, walk up onto the altar and stand at the podium.

I took the folded paper out of my coat pocket and opened it, laying it onto the Bible. I pressed out the wrinkles and folds so I could read it better. For a few moments I couldn't breathe or speak. I stood there, staring at the words I had written the day before. They frightened me. Not so much the words themselves, but what they meant. They meant I was saying goodbye to my husband forever.

I peered up at the church pews, trying to look over his coffin, but my eyes couldn't avoid it. There was Brandon. I was saying goodbye.

"Brandon, my husband, my love," I said. My eyes left the coffin and focused on the words I had written. "I cannot describe how much I miss you. The pain I feel. I want you to know that my life without you is empty."

Emotion choked my words and I had to stop for moment. I needed to get through this. I needed to say these things to him. If I cried, someone might feel sorry for me and come up to stop me. No, I needed to tell Brandon what he meant to me.

"No one can make me feel like you do," I said. I took a breath. "I miss your voice. Your hugs. Your kisses. I miss your phone calls every day. I would only have to think of you, think about calling you, and somehow you knew and you'd call me first." I looked down at his coffin. "What a loved we shared," I said. "We still do."

I looked over and saw my brother and sister watching me. They both had tears in their eyes. I looked down at the words I'd written. They blurred from my own tears. I wiped my eyes until the words were clear again. I continued.

"My heart is broken, my love," I said. "I am lost without you. You are an angel. No other man could ever replace you. You are beautiful inside and out."

I closed my eyes and I saw his smiling face. He was standing in our kitchen, pretending to be an announcer on television, a food program, talking about my tomato sauce. He laughed. It took all my strength not to cry out.

"Your heart was full of love," I said. "I have been so fortunate to have you in my life. My wonderful husband. My perfect love. I was always your princess. You understood my English when no one else could, just by looking into my eyes. You took care of me when I was sick. You gave me everything I could ever want. You are the love of my life. You will be in my heart always...until forever."

My mind went back to the two times we married, those days when I felt so high. The fall to the depths of that day left me not wanting to live past it.

"I will treasure you," I said in a whisper, "with everything I have, for the rest of my life. My great husband, my best friend...I will see you soon."

I took a breath. I'm not sure anyone heard my last words. It didn't matter anyway because I knew Brandon heard.

I read the last few words on the paper. "Forever, your wife."

I folded it back up, put it in my pocket and came down from the altar. Walking past his coffin was so difficult. Until I actually reached the first pew, where Rodolfo and Angela were, I didn't think I would make it. I didn't know it at the time, but what would be more difficult than that was when they carried his coffin away and put it in the ground, never again for me to see him.

CHAPTER 21

In the days following the funeral, I stayed upstairs in our bedroom most of the time and left Angela, Rodolfo and Lora alone downstairs. They would ask me repeatedly to come down, to eat, to talk to them, but I couldn't do any of those things. I lay in bed, sleeping, praying for Brandon to come back, begging God to take me so I could be with my husband.

One night I lay on the bathroom floor where I had found him, desperate to know what he saw when he was dying, as if somehow that was going to make me closer to him or bring him back. I started crying. I lay there, staring up at the room from the bathroom rug. Everything looked so scary and horrible from down here. The last moment of his life must have been awful for him. I cried and cried for what must have been hours, drifting in and out of sleep, dizzy from lack of food, desperately feeling suffocated with loneliness.

Then I heard it.

His voice whispered, "Don't cry, my love."

I fell silent and I focused everything I had on listening.

"Don't cry," his voice said again. "Get up."

And then his voice was gone, leaving me once again all alone.

○ ○ ○ ○ ○

Not long after the funeral, people started leaving, one by one. First Rodolfo, two days after Brandon was buried. A couple days later, Angela had to fly back to Italy too. My whole family was so far away. When she left, it was like I'd lost everyone again. Lora had to go back to Florida, too, and after she went to the airport, I found myself alone in that big house, more alone than I had ever known was possible.

I brought Brandon's ashes home and placed them in the living room on the fireplace mantel. He used to love being there, near the fire, relaxing, talking to me about our lives, about the things we'd been through, the things we wanted to do together in the future.

I stepped back and just stared at the urn. Maybe I'd thought that if I brought his ashes home it would feel he was home. But it didn't. I stood in the living room and felt surrounded by that massive, empty house. Why was I left with this big house? The size made it seem emptier. I couldn't possibly fill this much space with only my presence. What it was filled with instead was Brandon's absence.

I remained downstairs near his ashes as long as I could, avoiding the bedroom, *our* bedroom, where he would never be again, and the bathroom that looked into it, the bathroom where I'd found him.

· · · · ·

As the days blurred into weeks, I always dressed in black. Growing up in Italy I'd been taught that when a man dies, his wife wears only black for a full year. I knew this wasn't the custom in America, and probably wasn't the custom in Italy any longer, but in my heart that was what I needed to do. I owed that to Brandon.

I managed to leave the house, but mainly only to go in to work. And only because the business that Brandon had started needed me there. I didn't want to let him down by letting the business die. Doing the work was difficult. Inspiring clients, being upbeat for them, bringing energy to them was a torture. But I had to do it. And I needed it too. In a way, it gave me a break from the reality of my loss. If I focused on someone else's needs, I could forget my own.

I also needed it for income to survive. Bills arrived each week, things Brandon had always taken care of. Now I had to figure it all out and make sure everything was taken care of. The weight of everything came down on me. Mortgage, credit cards, utilities for both the house and the business, franchise fees, insurance premiums for several things, payroll, and more. They just kept coming, one after the other, never giving me any relief.

Many times I suffered panic attacks. I was so overwhelmed by how I would survive by myself with one paycheck that I couldn't breathe. I began to worry about running out of money. Brandon hadn't had life insurance. We'd discussed it, but we were both so young that we decided it wasn't necessary yet, nothing would happen. Now, without Brandon, the business was in jeopardy.

I needed to generate income the way Brandon had. I needed to sign up new clients. I needed to project a positive, happy attitude so the customers would want to come do business with Brandon's company. I had to do Brandon's work and my work. The reality of the business now being *mine* instead of *ours* was daunting.

Nights I went home and cried. I called out to him and demanded to know why he'd left me. I yelled at God for taking Brandon from me. I lay awake, trying to understand how this could have happened. Brandon was young and healthy. How could he have a heart attack and die? It made no sense. There were times when I questioned if all of this was really happening. There were times when I felt like I was losing touch.

I needed answers so I contacted his doctor's office and requested his medical records. When they came, I read every page, desperate to know how someone so strong and healthy could die so young. I stared in disbelief at the report that showed an abnormal EKG. Brandon had never mentioned this. His doctor, who was also my doctor, had never mentioned it.

His medical record also had a notation that he had been scheduled for a follow-up test, but he was a "no show." The notes went on to say that they had called him to reschedule, left messages, but he had never called back.

I scheduled an appointment for a physical with our doctor, not because I cared about my own health, but only because I wanted to talk to him.

I sat in the exam room, waiting, a hundred questions spinning in my head. When he walked in, I saw that him looking sad. But more than that. Troubled.

"How are you, Luisa?" he said, taking my hand in both of his. "Are you doing okay?"

I had no intention of talking about me.

"Why didn't you tell me that Brandon had a problem with his heart?" I asked.

My words hit him hard. He took a step back, almost as though he were staggering from a punch. He sat on the stool in front of me, his eyes moving to avoid mine.

"He shouldn't have had a heart attack," I said. "I should have known about this."

"We told Brandon that we needed to do more tests. He never followed up. I don't know the reason he didn't do them, but we couldn't force him."

"You never told me." I would have made sure Brandon did any tests he needed.

"We can't tell you because of the HIPPA laws."

"That's stupid!" I couldn't believe this. "I'm his wife. I have a right to know."

"Believe me, if we could have told you, we would have. But according to the law..."

"Are you serious?" I yelled. "You knew he was going to die and you didn't do anything to make sure he got the tests done that would save his life?"

"Luisa, that's not the way it was. We didn't know he was going to die. I didn't even know for sure that anything was wrong. Often people can have an irregular EKG and it turns out to be nothing. Sometimes a single test isn't conclusive. That's why we do more tests."

"It wasn't nothing! He died! Isn't that conclusive enough for you?"

I left.

I couldn't bear to hear his voice any longer. If he had done what he was supposed to, Brandon would be alive right now. If I had known that there had been problem, I would have convinced Brandon to get the tests done, and he would have because he loved me. If he had understood how serious this was, he would have taken whatever tests he needed to take. He wouldn't intentionally neglect this, knowing it could be serious. The doctor must not have explained it clearly.

I hated that man.

* * * * *

A few weeks later I received a letter from the doctor. It was short and to the point. He had decided to sell his practice. He would be leaving in a few months, and if I wanted to see the doctor who was buying his practice, I should call the office and make the arrangements. He thanked all of his patients and wished everyone well.

And me and Brandon?

CHAPTER 22

That night, alone in our home again, I wandered from room to room, the lights out. I could still smell Brandon's cologne in the living room. I remembered his laugh when I went to the living room. Upstairs, I felt the touch of his hands on my skin.

I cried again that night, as I did every night. I couldn't eat, couldn't sleep. I just kept thinking about Brandon and what had happened. If only I had another chance. If only the doctor had told me. If only I could go back in time. Everything would be different. The *if only*'s tormented me. The house tormented me. The studio tormented me. Loneliness tormented me. Life tormented me.

I went to the bathroom where I'd found him and as I had done many times sank to the floor in the same spot, desperate for a connection to him. I'd heard his voice once. I needed to hear him again. If I closed my eyes, I could see him lying there, see myself pressing on his chest, begging him not to die. I opened my eyes to the reality of the emptiness around me.

I should have died, not Brandon. I was older. He was so strong, so sure. I was the weak one, the one who needed him. How could he be the one to die?

Lying on the bathroom floor, the pain of losing my soul mate overwhelmed me, and I wailed, tears spewing. I pounded the tile floor, kicked at the sink cabinet and yelled at Brandon, at God. I couldn't go on without my husband, my love.

"I can't!" I yelled. "No!"

I sat alone in the kitchen on Sunday when the gym was closed. For hours I didn't move. I ate nothing. I didn't even go to church. I just thought and remembered.

The premonition I'd had months earlier, about my father dying, I had come to understand. The figure in the dream had been unclear. Of course, now I knew who it was. I should have been smarter. I should have understood the signs. God had been trying to tell me, but I didn't listen. I could have done something. I could have saved Brandon. I'd failed him.

Staring outside at the white covering of winter, I felt that my heart was like the snow outside, frozen over, lifeless. I started thinking about how much Brandon, unlike me, enjoyed the winter. For him to die during that time, what did that mean? Was that a good sign for him? For me, it made it so much worse. So much darkness, isolation. But maybe for him, it was a sign that his death was...

My train of thought was suddenly broken. Outside the window, on the back porch, I saw a shape in the snow. I got up from the stool at the kitchen island where I was sitting and walked to the window so I could see it clearly. Still questioning what was before my eyes, I went to the sliding door that opened onto the deck and pulled it open. The deck sprawled out before me, covered in white. There, at the edge of it, was a shape in the snow, the unmistakable form of a heart. But not just a heart. It was a heart separated in the middle with an unsteady line, as though it were broken into two pieces.

It took my breath away.

• • • • •

"It represents the two of you," she told me. "And it's also his heart and your heart, separately. Both of you are heartbroken."

I sat in the kitchen, my laptop on the granite island, staring at the medium who I had Skyped in hopes of getting answers, clarity, relief.

"He is still with you in spirit," the medium said.

"I want to feel his presence," I said.

"You will. Be patient. Right now all you feel is pain. When that subsides, you'll be able to feel him. He's there with you."

"How do I know? How do you know?"

"I can feel his intentions, his thoughts. Jewelry," she said.

"What about jewelry?"

"I'm getting a sense of the importance of jewelry to him. Do you know why I'm getting that? Does that mean something?"

"Yes!" I held up my wrist in front of the laptop camera. "He gave me this bracelet just a few days before he died and asked me never to take it off."

"Well, that does mean a lot to him."

"So he is here?"

"He's with you, Luisa."

"I need a sign."

"I think the snow and the jewelry are signs."

"I need more."

"What more do you need?"

"I want to feel him. I can't bear being without him. This house is so empty and lonely. I miss him so much. I need to know for sure that he's still with me. Ask him to move something in the house, this chair I'm sitting on, the microwave, something so I'll know for sure."

"I think what you're asking is too large," she told me.

"Please. I need it." I started to cry. "Please. Brandon," he said, looking out into the emptiness of the house. "Please give me a sign."

The medium was silent for a moment, her eyes closed. Then she opened them and looked at me through the computer.

"Put something small in the bedroom," she said. "He'll move it for you."

• • • • •

We ended the call. I went straight to the bedroom and placed a lipstick tube on the left side of the dresser. I made sure there was nothing else on top, nothing to interfere, only the photo of the two of us in Jamaica on the far right side. I made a mental note of exactly where the lipstick was. If it moved even an inch, I'd know.

Then I went to bed. I struggled to sleep, staring across the darkness at the dresser, hoping to see the lipstick slide. But it did not move. Finally I drifted to sleep. When I woke in the morning light, I sat upright and glared at the dresser. The lipstick was exactly where I'd left it. No sign. Hope slowly seeped away from me. Maybe I was all alone and would always be. If that was the case, I wasn't sure I wanted to go on. It would be so much better to be with Brandon.

Catholicism had ingrained in me that suicide was a mortal sin. If I killed myself, I would not go to Heaven where Brandon was. I would never see my love again. That realization, at the lowest moments, like right then, seeing the lipstick tube unmoved, that realization was the only thing keeping me from taking whatever pills I had to in order to kill myself.

○ ○ ○ ○ ○

I continued my routine as much as possible in the next days. Work, sleep, little else. Every evening I pulled into the garage and sat, trying to gather the strength to go inside the emptiness of our former home. Each time it got more difficult.

Every time I entered the bedroom I checked the lipstick. Every single time it was exactly where I'd left it. Every single time, my heart sank deeper into the darkness. The photo of us in Jamaica stared back at me, reminding me of how happy we'd been, how much I'd lost.

I stopped eating. I didn't care. I realized there was one way out, the only way out. I couldn't kill myself. But people died all the time from not eating and drinking, and they were not condemned for it. They were not denied Heaven.

CHAPTER 23

I pulled into the garage and left the motor running. Tears blurred my surroundings. As I climbed down out of the Escalade, I smelled exhaust in the garage and heard the engine ticking as it cooled. It made me so angry that I couldn't just let the fumes do the job and end my pain.

The house was silent. I couldn't stand it. My footsteps echoed off the tile floors and bare walls, reminding me of how empty the house was. I sipped Grand Marnier on the sofa, trying to disappear. Then, feeling strange, like maybe it was finally time, maybe God was finally going to take me, I went upstairs so it would happen in the bedroom.

"God, please let me make it to bed," I said out loud, my voice echoing in the emptiness.

Dizzy, I collapsed onto the bed. I felt a strange sensation, as though my soul was separating from my body. God was taking me.

"I'm ready," I said.

I had almost no strength left. The dizziness had become a noise in my head, a deafening cacophony. I squeezed my temples. It was painful.

"Take me, God," I shouted.

Relief. Salvation. I will have both at last, I hoped in desperation.

"God, is this my time?" I called out.

Through the noise in my head and the darkness surrounding me, I heard his voice. *Yes...*

I started crying, thankful that it was finally happening.

Wait, I wanted Brandon's ashes with me. But they were downstairs, on the fireplace mantel. I wasn't sure I could make it. But I wanted him there. I needed him. I pushed myself out of bed. My head was spinning. I had to hold the bed for a moment to steady myself, and then I found the strength to walk toward the door.

"God, please let me get the ashes," I said out loud.

As I passed the dresser to get to the door, I glanced down as I had done dozens of times in the last several days. It was automatic. My eyes went to the lipstick tube. To where it had always been, never moved.

Except tonight it was not there.

I stopped. Confused. That was the spot, wasn't it? My eyes wildly searched the darkness of the room, thinking at first that I was confused about where I'd left it, but then knowing that I was not mistaken. It had been there on the far left side and had remained on the far left side, day after day, unmoved, proving that I was alone.

Then I saw it.

"Oh, my God..." I couldn't move, just stared. I know I hadn't touched it. I hadn't moved it. It had to have been Brandon. And the place it moved to made complete sense.

I took a step toward it and leaned closer to make sure I was seeing it right. Yes. The lipstick tube had moved all the way across the dresser top and was now resting against the frame of the photo of Brandon and me in Jamaica.

I picked up the photo and stared at the two of us in one of the happiest times of our lives, when we were the closest we ever had been, the most in love. With my eyes fixed on the two of us smiling, I staggered backward to the bed and slowly sank down, sitting on the edge.

The image became blurry and I realized now that tears were flowing from my eyes. I squeezed my eyes closed, pressed the picture to my chest and settled backward until I was lying on the bed.

With my eyes still closed, I suddenly felt a presence in the room. Someone was beside me. I smelled Brandon's body. Not cologne this time, nothing like that. But rather him, his natural scent.

"My love," I whispered. I felt him touch my head and stroke my hair. My body shivered. I heard his voice.

"My love," he said back to me.

I gasped. "Oh, my God."

"When I was on the floor in the bathroom," he said, "why did you push so hard on my chest, my love?"

"I didn't want to lose you."

"You would try so hard for me?"

"I can't live without you," I said.

"Don't you know I'll always be with you?"

"I was afraid you wouldn't."

"No matter what, I'm always with you. I promise you."

I cried harder now, a mixture of sadness and happiness and fear and joy all together.

"Don't cry," Brandon said.

"I can't help it."

I felt his fingers on my cheek, wiping away the tears. "I don't want to see you sad."

"I miss you."

"I miss you, too."

I felt his body against mine now. The bed moved beneath me as he shifted his weight to get closer toward me. Then I felt him on top of me.

"My love, you're so beautiful," he said to me.

"I love you so much," I told him.

In an instant I felt him everywhere, around me, inside me, like a tidal wave of sensations and emotions washing over me. I was drowning in him, and I loved it. After being so long apart from each other, we were finally together, finally one again.

He would never leave me. Even death could not take away what we had between us.

I heard his voice over and over, "My love, you're so beautiful..."

CHAPTER 24

I started start going to church again. I didn't want to blame God for taking Brandon. I knew there must have been a reason, even though I still did not understand what that reason was. But my religion had helped me through many things in my life, and I needed to go back to that part of me to look for strength.

Every Sunday, Father Walsh's words from that altar guided me. Sometimes he seemed to be speaking directly to me. After mass, he stood at the doors of the church, greeting everyone as they left. The way he asked me how I was doing, I knew he cared. He wasn't just saying the words the way many people do. He cared. Knowing he cared gave me strength.

As did knowing that my friends Paula and Pat cared. Every day Paula would either call me or send me an email, checking in to see how I was. Repeatedly she offered to come over or told me to come over to her place. I always said no. I always wanted to be alone. But no matter how many times I declined, the next day she would reach out to me again. I just didn't want to be around people, to have to smile and pretend to be happy, to have to talk about things that didn't matter. I did enough of that at work and it was exhausting. It wasn't Paula, it was everyone.

Pat knew me well enough to ignore my wanting to be alone. She came over anyway, made sure I slept and ate. Sometimes she stayed with me all night so I wouldn't be by myself. She'd leave in the morning, go to work, live her life, and then come back again that night. She cared. Paula cared. Father Walsh cared.

The only one who didn't care was me.

I came to realize that my family cared about me, even though we were on different continents. Angela called me all the time and hearing from her meant everything to me. For the few minutes when we were on the phone together, I wasn't alone in the world. Her words soothed me and at the same time energized me. But after I hung up, I was alone again in that huge, empty house. Just me, my memories, my tears.

The dark winter days were smothering me.

Snow dumped more problems onto my life. Without Brandon, I not only had to run the business by myself, but I also had to shovel the snow. I had a plow clear the driveway, but everything else—the sidewalk, the front entrance, the area near the garage so I could get my car out—all fell on me. When Brandon was there, he'd do all that. If I came outside to help him, he'd send me back inside.

"It's too cold," he would say. "I don't want you doing this kind of work. I'll take care of it, my love."

But now I had no one to send me back inside.

Storm after storm in the weeks after Brandon died I went out and shoveled. In March one new storm covered New England. I woke up to a foot of snow blocking my garage doors, with more snow still falling. But I had to get to work. I trudged outside to dig a path for my car to get out of the garage. It was a wet snow. Each shovelful I heaved out of the way seemed to weigh fifty pounds. My fingers quickly became numb from the cold. My body ached. More snow kept falling. And I kept digging. But the snow was endless. The winter was endless. Bleak, dark, difficult days that never ended. And I had to face it all alone, no hope for things to get better, just me against a world that had turned against me.

As I stuck the shovel into the snow and heaved another mound off to the side, I couldn't take it any longer. I threw the shovel as far as I could and screamed into the falling snow, no words, just howls of anger and frustration and sadness. When I had spent all my strength screaming, I sank down into the mound of snow and wept.

· · · · ·

One Saturday morning in early spring my phone rang. I was already awake, lying in bed. The snow still hadn't melted outside. Sunrise brought chilled air that made me not want to crawl out from under the covers. I answered the phone.

"How are you, Luisa?" It was my sister, Angela.

I looked around the empty bedroom and felt the aloneness that had persisted since Brandon was taken from me. It wasn't fair that God took him. Brandon should have been here with me right now.

"How am I?" I said. "How do you think?"

"I know you're not happy. You have to think about other things or you'll never get over this."

"Get over it? You sound like an American."

"I mean you have to live your life again, Luisa."

"I am living," I said.

"Barely."

I couldn't disagree. Instead, I said, "Why did God take him, Angela? This isn't right."

She told me all the reasons, justifications that I'd heard a thousand times before from a dozen other people, all the ways I was supposed to think in order to accept what happened and move on. But I couldn't accept it. I couldn't move on. How can a person simply move on from the one love of their life? We'd been through so much and came out stronger, closer, more in love. Only to have it all ripped away. Move on? The only move on I could imagine myself doing was moving on to the same place Brandon was.

But then Angela said something else, something that went straight to my heart, something that hurt.

"Listen to me, Luisa. Please. I know it's hard, but you need to let him go, not just for you, but even more so for him."

I didn't understand. "For him?"

"Yes, for him."

"I can't," I said, falling back on the words I'd said over and over, the thought that never left me. "I can't."

"You have to. You're holding him. Don't you understand? You're holding him."

"What does that mean, I'm holding him?" Her words started to anger me. "I wish to God I could hold him."

"No, you're holding him from going through the light. He needs to go to heaven, Luisa, but he won't until you let him go."

"I can't let him go!"

"You have to."

"I can't. I don't want to be without him."

"If you love him, if you truly love him, you have to let him go through the light. It's not fair to him. He needs to get to Heaven. You're stopping him."

"No." I didn't want to believe I was doing that to him. I never wanted to hurt him in any way. "No," I repeated.

"Luisa, let him go. For him. For you, too. Let him go."

I realized that she was right, and all I could do was cry.

· · · · ·

When I hung up with Angela, I called Father Walsh. I needed to see him. For me, he was the embodiment of the world Brandon had gone to, the clarity of what God wanted. I needed help seeing the correct path to take. If anyone could shed light on the answers, my hope was that it was Father Walsh.

Though he didn't usually work in his office Saturday mornings, he told me to come over to the rectory right away. An hour later I was sitting in his office, sobbing and asking for guidance. He told me that Angela was right. I did need to let Brandon go.

But he was more concerned about me, about how my holding onto Brandon was affecting me. He worried that I had given up on life. I needed to let my husband be with God, true. But I needed to do it, not just for Brandon, but also for me.

Father Walsh and I talked for an hour and a half. His words brought me peace. He said God would help me if I let Him. I left, desperate for God to take me by the hand and show me how to survive this loss.

I started volunteering at the church, donating to the charities. They had a group for widows. I supported them and tried their meetings, even though I was half the age of most of them. Being in the church, having that community to fill some of the emptiness left by Brandon's death, did give me a little strength. I felt strong enough to talk to other people going through depression and try to give them encouragement.

Even though this helped a little, the pain of losing Brandon remained. I let him go, let him pass through the light.

But I was in the pits of depression.

. . . . .

Being involved in the Church was helpful, but as time wore on and my depression remained, I knew I needed professional help. I recognized that this was too much for me to handle on my own. I remembered how difficult it had been for me when my mother had died. And in those days, in Naples, people didn't get professional help. If you even mentioned a psychiatrist or a therapist, people would think you were crazy. But I was a long way from the Naples of my youth, both in physical location and in time.

When I had moved to Massachusetts years earlier, I had contacted a clinical psychologist to help me with some unresolved feelings having to do with my mother's death. I realized it was time to call her again.

I started going to see Cindy weekly, talking about everything I was going through, all the feelings I was having. I even told her about the "event" in our bedroom that night, when I felt Brandon there with me. I hadn't discussed it with anyone else. I didn't know what they would think of me. But I trusted Cindy. I also needed to talk to someone about it.

As I explained to her what had happened that night, I watched her expression. All I saw was attentiveness, concern. "Do you think I'm crazy?" I asked.

She smiled. "One thing I can tell you for certain, you're not crazy."

I knew I wasn't crazy, but hearing her, a professional, tell me gave me an incredible relief.

"Could I have imagined the whole thing?" I asked.

"Luisa, only you know the answer to that. What do you think?"

"It seemed very real to me."

"There's you answer."

"So then what am I supposed to do?"

"What do you want to do?" Cindy asked me.

"Sometimes there are moments," I said, "when all I want to do is die so I can be with Brandon."

"I know how terrible it feels to lose someone who's so close to you."

"He was my whole life. Without him, I don't have a life. If it wasn't such a bad sin, such a bad act against God, I would have done it."

Cindy nodded. From her expression I knew she cared. She said, "There are times in our lives that aren't easy."

"There are times that are too hard," I said.

"Yes, there are."

"The only thing that gets me through the days is thinking how I'm going to make Brandon proud of me."

"Well, that's what you should do then. That's good enough. That's plenty."

"But it never gets better. Sometimes I can't even bear to face the next day, with nothing changing."

"Just get through each day. Let tomorrow come tomorrow. One day's enough at one time. Just take care of today. I promise you, eventually the tomorrows will get better."

. . . . .

She listened to all of my stories of sadness, and even though I knew she was being paid to do this, I could tell that she genuinely cared. Her advice helped me through the darkness. From talking to me about making sure that I ate properly and slept the right amount of hours, to figuring out why God separates people who love and need each other so much, the weekly visits with her gave me strength to go on.

I talked to her about the difficulties of returning each day to the house I had shared with Brandon, about my feelings of loneliness at the same time that I didn't want to be with other people, about the problems and the successes I had at the studio, the thing that was, in a way, my reason for living. I still needed to make it a success for Brandon.

"And for you?" Cindy asked. "Couldn't making it a success be for you, too? For both of you?"

I shrugged. I couldn't think about it in those terms. Not at that moment, anyway. But afterwards, when I was at work, putting in sixteen hours a day to make sure it was successful, increasing the number of clients beyond what Brandon and I had imagined it would be at this point,

I did let myself feel proud of what I was doing. Maybe what I was achieving at the studio could, in part, be for me, too.

The sad thing was, as well I was doing at work, without Brandon, I had no one to share it with. And alone, it didn't have much meaning. Alone, life had little meaning.

CHAPTER 25

Fifteen months after Brandon died, I opened my email to see a message from the corporate offices of Fitness Together, the franchise I owned, announcing the annual franchisee conference in Florida. In the past, Brandon and I had gone together each year. It had usually been a great networking and learning experience for our business and a wonderful time away for the two of us.

The previous year, I'd been so distraught by Brandon's death that I hadn't even noticed it was conference time. Not that I would have gone without him. This year, though, I wondered if attending would be a good step to take. The thought of actually doing it terrified me.

When I went to see Cindy for my weekly therapy session, I told her about the conference and my considering going.

"I think that would be great for you," she said.

"I'm not sure if I'm ready."

"How would you feel different if you were ready?"

"I don't know. I wouldn't be so scared."

"Being afraid isn't what tells us we can or should do something. Fear is only an obstacle, the same as being tired can be an obstacle or bad weather or a broken leg are obstacles. They are things that we can overcome, not things that tell us if we're ready or not, or whether or not we should do something. The healing process involves taking steps. Some steps are simple, some are more challenging. This one might be more challenging, but it is another step. You know you've taken many other steps, Luisa. This is one more."

I understood all of that already. But it was easier to understand it and say it than it was to actually do it. "I know it would be good for me to get out of my comfort zone, and that is definitely out of my comfort zone. I was thinking, maybe Brandon would want me to go."

"I'm more interested in hearing what you want, not what you think Brandon wants."

"What I want?"

"Yes. That's what matters."

I wasn't sure how to say what I thought. I sat forward and looked at her.

"Cindy, life doesn't mean anything to me anymore. I don't want anything. I'm not even sure I want to be alive."

She reached over and placed her hand on mine. "Luisa, I think life has more meaning to you than you realize."

"No, it doesn't."

"Then why do you get up every morning and go to work and spend so many hours and continue growing your business?"

"I do that for Brandon. Because the studio meant the world to him."

"That's not the reason."

"Yes, it is," I said.

"Why do you come here then? You come here for Brandon too?"

"I come here because it helps me to talk with you."

"Exactly. It helps *you*. Not Brandon. I think that if you look real hard, you may see that other things you do are also for you. You're trying to put your life back together, and that's for you."

"I want him to be proud," I said.

"Yes, I know. I get it that the studio was something he started with you and so it means a lot, and you want to honor him. But you also have to do it for you. To be proud of yourself. And maybe you can't see it, but I can. You dress well. You put on makeup. You always look good."

"I have to for the business."

"No, you don't. You do it because you decided that it matters. You do things for Brandon, there's no question. But you also do things for you, and you do it because even though you are deeply sad and mourning the loss of your one true love, your life does matter."

I couldn't answer. Maybe she was right. I wasn't sure anymore.

"So maybe Brandon does want you to go," she said. "But what do you want to do?"

"Why do you turn it back to me? *You* tell me, what should I do?"

"You know the answer that is right for you, Luisa. There isn't a wrong thing to do. What do you feel?"

"I don't know what I feel sometimes."

"Well, think about it. What do you feel right now?"

"I think maybe Brandon might want..."

"Luisa," she said, raising her hand to stop me. "Not what do you think Brandon might want. I want to know what you think, what you want?"

I hesitated, trying to know what I should do. It was difficult for me to imagine taking any trip without Brandon, let alone a trip we used to take together. But then again, it had been difficult for me to imagine running our studio alone, making a life in our home alone. Over the last year, I had gradually come to understand that I was stronger than I'd thought. I could survive a lot. Possibly I could even thrive...

"Maybe I can go," I said.

Cindy smiled. "Why not?"

· · · · ·

Why not? The closer I came to getting on the plane and flying down there, the more reasons I came up with for why not. Who was going to take care of the business? What if there were a problem at the house and I wasn't there to take care of it? What if there were a hurricane in Florida? What if...what if...what if...?

But I had made up my mind that I'd go. I went shopping for some new clothes, colorful clothes. The year of wearing black was over. Brandon would like me to wear colors again. As I tried on different dresses, I looked at myself in the mirror and realized that it felt good to care about the way I looked. I began to enjoy dressing up again.

The business continued to do well and shortly before it was time to take the trip, I received the news that my studio was the top revenue producer in the entire country for the previous month. The trainers and I celebrated in the studio. I saw how thrilled they were. I said that Brandon would be proud of all of them. They congratulated me. It really did feel good. And that feeling helped me as I boarded that plane to Florida. Tears were in my eyes, but underneath I knew I had a strength in me and I needed to rely on that strength.

· · · · ·

Being in Fort Walton Beach brought back memories. I had always traveled with Brandon. We were inseparable. Without him, I felt out of place. Even just checking into the hotel. He always took care of everything. But now I was on my own.

As I filled out the paperwork and handed the woman behind the counter my credit card, I told myself that I could do this. Life had been better with Brandon, but it did not have to come to an end without him. Just as the business didn't close and the house didn't fall apart, my life could continue. Coming here was a step toward being alive again. I would never stop loving Brandon, never stop missing him, never stop wishing he were by my side, experiencing whatever I was experiencing.

But I could feel alive again. Perhaps not happy. I still was not able to imagine myself feeling that. But I could at least feel something approaching contentment.

I went up to my room and unpacked. The franchisees were invited to a welcome party out by the pool. I went out onto the balcony and saw people gathering below. Everyone was dressed up, the men in sports coats, the women in short dresses and heels. A DJ played club versions of pop music, competing with the sound of the waves coming from the beach. I wasn't sure I should go. I was in no mood to mingle and make small talk. But I had come here as part of healing, of rebuilding my life. I needed to go down there and meet the other studio owners.

I had no idea what to wear. For things like this, Brandon always helped me decide. I used to love trying on outfits and getting his responses. On my own, I couldn't make up my mind. I picked up my cell phone and I called Lora, Brandon's mother. She had good taste. And she was one of the few people I knew I could count on. She told me to relax and assured me that we would pick the right dress together. Then I described everything I'd brought with me.

"Definitely the ivory dress," she said.

"You think so?"

"Definitely. With your skin tone, it'll be perfect."

"Okay, if you think so. Thanks, Lora."

"And have a good time," she told me. "Enjoy yourself, for God's sake."

"I'll try."

At first I felt uncomfortable, but as I met people I knew from previous conferences, I began to feel more comfortable. Many people didn't recognize me because I'd changed my hair color. Everyone was so kind. They kept complimenting me on how good I looked. If only they knew how much sadness I had inside. But tonight I let the happiness of the event take over. I ate and drank and even danced a little. By the time I went back to my room, I felt happy that I'd gone. A few months ago, I would not have been able to imagine me at a party. This was another small step on my road to healing.

The last night there, the owner of the company invited me to sit at his table at the award banquet. He was very kind to me and made sure I was enjoying myself. It wasn't easy being there, but I was beginning to enjoy being out again, doing things other than work, talking with people.

"You're a strong woman," he told me.

I was surprised that he'd say that. "Why do you say that?" I asked.

"It's obvious. I can see it. Other people said the same thing."

"People are talking about me?"

"People are always talking. We missed you last year. Now you're back. It was a tough year for you. I know that. Everyone knows that. I can see how you're doing now. And I know how your studio is doing. I know about April. Congrats."

"Thank you."

"I'm impressed."

I felt myself blush. "Thank you again."

"It's all justified. Anyway," he said, "I want to see you up there accepting an award."

"Maybe you will. I want to be the number one studio."

"I'll bet you do it, too."

Before I left for Boston, a man from the corporate public relations department asked if he could interview me. He said he'd heard about my story and thought I would have something to say that might be helpful to other people going through difficult times. It would also be inspiring to other franchisees, giving them that extra push to get their studios to be more successful. If I could do it going through the loss of my husband and business partner, imagine what they could do.

As I left Florida, I thought about how proud Brandon must be. I knew he had been watching and listening to all of it. I had vowed that I would treasure the business that he had started and given to me, and as difficult as it had been, I had not only kept it going, but I had made it even more successful. I did it for him and because of him.

Sitting on the plane, this time not crying, I closed my eyes and whispered, "This is for you, my love."

CHAPTER 26

"I'm afraid," I told Cindy.

"Of what?" the therapist asked me.

"Of being with them. They made me very unhappy."

"That was before. Your happiness isn't up to them anymore. Your happiness is up to you, Luisa."

"Maybe it's not the right time."

"There's not going to be a better time."

"I don't know," I said.

"Think of it as part of your therapy," Cindy said. "I'll be good for you. Your family has been a missing piece in your life ever since you left Italy twenty years ago."

"I had Brandon. There was nothing missing."

"Brandon loved you, there's no question about it. And you loved him. But he couldn't be everything for you."

"Yes, he was."

"He couldn't fill the hole left by your family, even if he and you wanted him to. Many different people make up our social circle. Different people are there at different times, but no one person can be all of them. Just as your father could not take the place of your mother, Brandon never could take the place of your brothers and sisters. Or of your father."

"I'm still not good with my father," I said. He hadn't come after Brandon died. He hadn't been supportive at any time in my life.

"And maybe that relationship will never be a good one," Cindy said. "But don't miss out on the rest of your family to avoid him. I want you to go. Think of it as part of your therapy."

"That's what you said about going to Florida."
"Was I wrong? Was it a bad thing to do?"
"No."
"All right then."
I sighed. "So I have to go?"
"Yes." Cindy leaned forward. "Something's going to happen there," she said. "I don't know exactly what, but something."
"Something good or something bad?"
Cindy smiled. "Would I send you to do something bad? Go, Luisa. Go and heal."

• • • • •

My oldest brother Paolo was a pilot. He helped me get the tickets to fly to Rome, connecting to Bari in the "heel" of Italy, where he had a place on the beach. I thought it would be a good distraction to spend some time there, away from the stresses at work, away from the memories at the house, away from the life I had in Boston. He had a wife, who I got along with well, and children I looked forward to spending time with. They were thrilled to have me visit.

I stopped at Barnes & Noble on the way home from work one evening and bought a couple paperback books. My plan was to lie out on the beach under the sun and just relax. Southern Italy in August is hot and humid. Most Italians headed to the beach. I had been one of them for the first two decades of my life. I missed that world and for the first time in many years I was looking forward to going back to my Italian roots.

As the day approached to get on the plane and go there, I began have panic attacks. I wasn't sure I'd be able to handle it, all the kids, the confusion. My father. I thought about canceling.

When I called Angela and told her I might not be coming, she said, "Paolo's going to be upset. Francesca and the kids, too. They really want you to visit. Try," Angela said. "If after you're here you change your mind, you can turn around and fly back. But if you don't try, you'll never know. Maybe it's the best thing for you."

She was right. At least I had to try.

• • • • •

During the ride to the airport, tears flowed out of my eyes. I tried to hold it in, tried not to let the driver see, but I couldn't stop and I was sure he noticed. This trip was one of the most difficult things I had done since Brandon's death. Sure it was another step. But it did not feel like a small step, as everything else had until now.

I arrived at the terminal, my body shaking. Flights to Europe leave Boston in the evening so the airport wasn't crowded, just the passengers for my flight. Still, I struggled to breathe and to hold in my tears because of the anxiety I felt. I still wasn't convinced I should be going, but as I got in line to check in for the flight, I realized that every time I was nervous about going somewhere, it always turned out to be the best thing for me, often changing my life for the better. With that in mind, I decided that this trip would be the same. Something good would happen.

On the plane, after the captain had turned out the lights, I began to miss Brandon terribly. I'd been without him for eighteen months and still the pain in my heart was as sharp as it had been the day he died. I closed my eyes and began to weep. I eventually drifted off. When we arrived in Rome the next morning, my eyes felt puffy. My body felt jetlagged. I had to rush to catch a connecting flight to Bari.

Being in Italy felt both comfortable and uncomfortable. I'd lived in the United States for more than two decades, and some of the customs there suited me better, but at heart I would always be Italian, and being in Rome, hearing my first language being spoken and yelled and laughed, seeing the open emotions in people, made me feel like I belonged.

But also I was getting close to my family, and to my past, and all the fears I had were now magnified. I tried not to think about that, tried to concentrate on getting through customs and immigration, finding the gate that I had to go to for my connecting flight, listening to the announcements to hear the boarding call.

When I got on the plane, my heart raced. I'm really doing this, I thought. I'm really going there. I found my seat and sat down. It took a couple minutes to put away my carry-on bag, buckle my seatbelt and get out something to read to distract me.

"Luisa," a voice said.

I looked up. Paolo's smiling face hung above me.

"Paolo?" I tried to jump up to hug my brother, but the seatbelt held me down. We both laughed as I unbuckled the seatbelt and finally hugged him. It was so good to see him, so comforting to feel my oldest brother holding onto me. "Are you flying the plane?" I asked.

"No. I'm a passenger like you. I'm on my way back from a flight to Paris. I'm up there," he said, gesturing to the front. "But we're flying together. Don't worry. I'm with you the rest of the way."

When he left to go back to his seat, I cried again, but this time they were tears of joy.

· · · · ·

Paolo's house was located a mile from the beach. From his patio I could hear the Ionian Sea and I longed to walk on the sand and feel the warm surf washing over me. That would come later. First I wanted to spend some time with my brother and his wife, Francesca. She left us alone for a few minutes while she went inside to get cold drinks. Paolo and I sat, taking in the sun and the cooling breeze.

"I'm really glad you came, Luisa," Paolo said.

"I am too."

"Anything we can do to make your stay better, you let me know, okay?"

I smiled. "Thank you." But I didn't need much. Just their company and the place would do wonders, I was sure.

Paolo glanced back at the door of the house to see if Francesca was coming back yet. When he didn't see her, he turned back to me and spoke in a whisper.

"Listen, while you're here I'm going to introduce you to a lot of good people."

"I'm really fine with just the family."

"It's good to meet people," he said. "Especially one person I know."

I looked at him more closely. He had that look I remembered from our childhood, that he was up to something.

"What person?" I asked.

"He's single."

"Paolo!" That wasn't where my thoughts were right now.

He gestured with his hand for me to speak more softly and said, "Maybe you want to go out on a date one night." He shrugged and looked at me for a reaction.

I didn't answer. I just looked back at the sea.

"Or even have a one night stand," he said.

I whipped my head back toward him. "I can't believe you're saying this to me. I didn't come here for that."

"All right, but you're old enough to do whatever you want."

I covered my ears. I didn't want to hear any more.

But he wasn't finished. "It's your life," he said. "You do whatever will make you happy."

"I will."

"You will have the one night stand?"

The look on his face made me laugh. "No!" I said. "I will do what I want."

Francesca came out of the house now with the drinks.

"Who's thirsty?" she asked.

I pointed to Paolo.

"He definitely needs to put something in his mouth so he won't talk so much."

. . . . .

Over the next few days Paolo and Francesca introduced me to many of their friends. Much to my surprise I enjoyed meeting them. It kept me from thinking. Every night we went to a party. Italian parties involve eating, some drinking, and a lot of dancing. It had been too long since I'd danced like this. It made me feel free. I was so thankful to be surrounded by such wonderful people. I couldn't believe how foolish I'd been to feel anxious about coming here. Now I never wanted to leave.

Paolo came over to me one night just as I finished a dance. He had that look on his face again, the childhood, up to something wrong look.

"Come here," he said, taking my hand and pulling me toward a table.

"Where are we going?"

"I want you to meet someone."

I knew right away what he was up to, but before I could stop him we were at the table. A tall, tanned man dressed in white stood up when he saw me. A few other people were sitting there, but my attention went directly to him. He stared at me with the kind of look I'd seen in men before, the look I'd always avoided. But something about this night, the sea air, the wine I'd had, the hours of dancing, lowered my resistance. For the first time, I didn't mind his appraising eyes on me.

"Luisa, this is Erasmo Fiorentino," Paolo said.

Erasmo came around the table, hugged me and kissed both of my cheeks. His hands were warm grasping my shoulders. He smelled of a sweet, musky cologne.

"It's such a pleasure to meet you, Luisa," he said.

I just nodded.

"You can call me Mimmo. Your brother has told me so much about you." He gestured toward the table. "Why don't you sit down and have some wine with us?"

The others at the table said, yes, join them.

My instinct was to say no, but Paolo answered for me and practically pulled me into the seat next to Mimmo. He seemed a decent man, strong, but polite and refined. He kept trying to talk to me, but I really wasn't in the mood. I stayed only long enough to be polite, and then I excused myself and walked away.

A couple nights later at another party, I ran into Mimmo again. I didn't accept his offer to have a drink with him, making the excuse that some people on the other side of the house we were at were waiting for me. In truth, I thought he was good looking and he seemed kind, but I wasn't sure I was ready to get to know him, or anyone else, better right now.

I met him at another party. We laughed about running into each other so often. Paolo and Francesca kept encouraging me to go out on a date with him, to let him pursue me, but I kept saying that I wasn't interested.

"Is there someone else you like?" Paolo asked. "I can make it..."

"No, please," I said, laughing. "Don't do anything. Just let me go at my own pace."

"He's a doctor, you know."

"I don't need a doctor. I'm fine."

"That's not what I meant."

"I know what you meant. I'm not ready, Paolo."

· · · · ·

Days were spent on the beach. The sun felt so good. Even in summer in Massachusetts it was rare for me to find time to take the sun and nearly impossible for me to get out to the beach.

The parties every night were so much fun. Italian life was so much different from American life. Even at a party people felt deeply connected to the people around them. They knew how to have fun. They drank without getting drunk. And food was always at the center, fresh, tasty, healthy food.

As my two weeks were drawing to an end, Paolo and Francesca came to me. My brother said, "Luisa, we really loved you staying with us."

"It's been wonderful," Francesca said. "And the kids are in love with you."

"For me it has been the best time I could have ever asked for. Thank you so much."

"We'd love it if you could stay another week," Paolo said.

"I don't know," I said.

Francesca said, "It would be great if you could."

"I have to get back to work. The studio can't run itself."

"For one more week?" Paolo said. "It's been okay so far, right? What's another week?"

"I'd love to, but I'm not sure I can. Let me think about it, okay?"

"Of course. Think about it. But don't think too long. The longer we wait the harder it'll be to find a ticket. I'll try, though. Let me know by tomorrow at midnight at the latest, and I'll do everything I can to change your tickets."

"I'll let you know."

The next night we were at a dinner party and I was seated next to Mimmo the whole time. He made sure I had anything I wanted and he talked to me about my life and my trip to Italy. I didn't like talking about myself much and turned the topic of the conversation back to him. He was a doctor, I found out, divorced and had two children, an eight year old daughter and an eighteen year old son who lived with Mimmo's ex-wife. He was also very kind and easy going. His disposition put me at ease. I enjoyed dinner with him. It was sort of the date with him I'd been avoiding for so long. I realized I had had nothing to be afraid of all along.

After dinner, as we sipped the last of our wine, he said, "You know, your brother would really like you to stay."

"He told you?"

"He mentioned it. He said he doesn't see you often and loves having you here."

"I love being here."

"So then you should just stay."

"I don't know."

"What is there to know?" Mimmo said. "He and Francesca want you to stay. You want to stay. We all want you to stay."

"*We* all?" I said.

He smiled. "You're very popular."

I didn't know what to say. I looked down at my wine glass, feeling nervous by the attention. "I don't know," I said. "It's probably too late to change anyway. It might cost too much or there might not be any seats left to go back a week later."

"You won't know until you try."

I looked up. The way he looked at me made me feel things I hadn't felt in a long time. I felt like a woman, like I was fully alive. But I still wasn't sure this was the right thing to do.

"I have to get back to my home and my business," I said.

"That's too bad."

"Yes," I said into my wine. I looked at my watch. It was nearly midnight.

He noticed and said, "You have to decide, Luisa."

I took a sip of wine and looked across the room at Paolo and Francesca, laughing and talking with other guests. I really did hate to leave them, to leave here where I felt part of the world again, part of a family. I turned back to the intriguing man sitting beside me. He was staring at me, eager for an answer.

"What?" I said.

He looked straight into my eyes and this time I couldn't look away. "Luisa, don't go," he said. "Change your ticket. Stay." The conviction and insistence in his tone impressed me.

He didn't wait for me to answer. He stood up and took hold of my hand. "Let's go tell your brother," he said.

"It's probably too late," I said as I stood up. "He might not even be able to change it any longer."

"Let him try."

We walked over to Paolo who was happy to see the two of us together.

"Can you see if you can change my ticket?" I asked him.

"You're going to stay?"

"If you can change it and it doesn't cost too much, yes, I'll stay."

He jumped up and took out his cell phone. "Give me a minute. I'll call now. Be right back." He rushed toward the house, dialing before he even got inside away from the noise of the party.

The music played into the night, carried by the sea breeze. Francesca and Angela pulled me away from the tables to dance. The air was hot and humid. I was dripping with sweat but enjoying every minute. Paolo emerged from the house, beaming. He waved to me as I was dancing then he gave me the thumbs up and smiled.

I said, "Oh, my God," feeling crazy that I was doing this, but at the same time happy about it. Something inside me told me that this was the right thing, that something good would happen.

CHAPTER 27

The night I decided to stay longer in Italy, I dreamed about Mimmo.

The next day I went for a walk on the beach. I loved taking long walks in the sand. I wanted to get as much of it as possible before I went back because I knew that at home there was no beach for me to walk on like this. While I was walking, I ran into Mimmo.

"I think you're following me," he said, smiling. "Where are you going?"

"Just walking."

"Would you like some company?"

I shrugged and continued walking. He came along. He asked me about my business and what life was like in Massachusetts. I didn't talk much, just short answers. He told me about his work as a doctor and about his eight year old daughter. He had been through a difficult divorce the year before and was still affected by it.

"Paolo told me about your husband," he said.

I just nodded.

"It's very difficult losing someone you love."

"More difficult than you can imagine," I said. "He was my whole life."

"He must have been a special man."

"Yes, he was."

I told him some of the stories of our life, how we met, sneaking onto the Marine base, moving to America. I was surprised at how he listened, how he was interested. I told him how there had been struggles too, but we'd overcome them and our love was stronger because of it. I told him how devastating Brandon's death was to me.

"And you found him?" he said.

I nodded. I had to bite down to keep from crying. "I tried to save him," I said.

The image of Brandon on the bathroom floor rushed into my head. I saw my hands pressing down on his chest. Not hard enough, not fast enough, not right somehow. Because I couldn't keep his heart beating.

"I failed," I whispered.

I didn't think he heard me with the sounds of the waves beside us, but he stopped, took my arm and gently turned me toward him.

"You didn't fail, Luisa."

"I didn't save him."

"You did everything you could."

"I didn't save him."

"It's not your fault."

"I didn't save him," I said again. "If I had done CPR better or gone upstairs sooner or paid attention to how he looked, he wouldn't have died."

"That's not true."

"Yes it is. He counted on me. We counted on each other and I let him down."

"You tried to save his life."

"I let him die!" I was shaking now. Tears streamed down my cheeks. It took all my strength not to weep.

He grasped my shoulders. "Luisa, listen to me. You did everything you could."

I shook my head. "You don't know."

"I'm a doctor, remember? I do know. If anyone knows what can be done to save someone and what can't, I know. It's not your fault."

"I didn't save him."

"You did the most anyone could have done. You can't see heart disease in someone. You can't predict when someone is going to have a heart attack. And you can't force the heart to do what you want it to do, no matter how well you do CPR."

"I should have..."

"Luisa. Listen to me. His death isn't your fault."

I stared at him, seeing in his eyes how certain he was. In that moment

I couldn't control myself. My tears exploded and I fell against him.

"But I didn't want him to die," I said, weeping.

"I know."

"He shouldn't have died."

"It's not your fault, Luisa."

"Why did he die? Why did God take him from me?"

Mimmo held me and whispered over and over that it would be all right, that it wasn't my fault. In the way his arms surrounded me, I felt protected, I felt that he really cared about me. We barely knew each other, but I felt safe crying in his arms. I had not allowed myself to feel that way in a very long time.

· · · · ·

I was not looking for another man, could not imagine ever being with anyone other than Brandon, but destiny put Mimmo in my life at that moment, and though our relationship was not physical, not romantic, I spent much of that last week in Italy with him. We had dinner a few times, walked on the beach, went to a party.

He fed me one night in a restaurant, which made me smile. I felt like a little girl again. Another night he ordered all kinds of seafood and we laughed as we tasted it all. Being with him was like a medicine that gradually made you feel better.

The last night we had dinner together again, and afterward we picked up his daughter Nicole and the three of us went to the beach. I took off my high heels. Mimmo rolled up his linen pants. The three of us walked under the night sky, gazing out over the Mediterranean at the stars glistening in the sky. Waves washed in. Nicole and I tried to jump out of the way. We were wearing short dresses and the cool water splashed our legs. A few times we splashed Mimmo by mistake, soaking his pants. He chased us. We all laughed.

Nicole ran off to chase a sea gull, laughing. I stopped, suddenly filled with guilt that I was having such a good time. I stared at a wave washing ashore. Mimmo came over and put his arm around me.

"It's all right," he said.

I stared at him. "What do you mean?"

"It's all right to be happy."

I shook my head. "My husband..." I started to say, but my words trailed off.

"Luisa, do you think he would want you to be unhappy?"

"It's wrong."

"No, it isn't. Your husband loved you. He would want you to be happy. If it were the other way around, you would want him to be happy, right?"

I nodded.

"So it has nothing to do with him not wanting you to be happy," Mimmo said. "He does. The one that needs to want you to be happy again"—he put his finger under my chin and lifted my face until I was staring into his eyes—"is you," he said. "Are you ready to be happy again?"

· · · · ·

The day I left for Boston, Mimmo couldn't come to the airport because he had too many patients. But in between patients he called me, asking how I was, did I need anything, when was I coming back, then he'd hurry off to see another patient. Then the phone would ring again and it would be Mimmo. He had a few minutes before the next patient to talk to me. I thought it was funny, and cute, and romantic. He called three times before my flight left.

The trip back to Boston was long and filled with mixed feelings. I was going back to the life that was familiar, the life I'd built with Brandon. But I felt a new strength, like a part of me was reborn. For so long I had thought my life was over, and I had lived every day that way, never imagining the long term, never envisioning my being happy again as part of it.

But as I stared out the window of the jet at the clouds, I honestly felt the seeds of happiness growing inside me. But with that happiness was a new sadness. I was already missing Mimmo. We lived five thousand miles apart. We had separate lives. I had enjoyed being with him, and I dreaded being alone again.

When I got back to Massachusetts and arrived at my house, the size and emptiness of it struck me. All of this massive emptiness was mine, and mine alone. Here, though, I sensed Brandon's presence. Not in a bad way. It was a strange mixture of reassurance that he was watching over me and loneliness that he wasn't physically with me any longer, and never would be.

I went up to the bedroom, left the suitcase by the dresser and sat on the edge of the bed. As always, I felt him there. I took a deep breath and let it out slowly. I closed my eyes. Like this I could always feel his presence stronger.

I had to ask him.

"Brandon, my love," I said. "Are you happy with my new relationship?"

In the silence of the room, I listened to his answer and began to cry.

CHAPTER 28

It was warm for late October.

I left work early on Tuesday. Things had been hectic for weeks now, fourteen hour days most of the time. The business was doing well, but being the sole owner meant that everything fell on me. I'd promoted Garren to manager and handed over some of the responsibility, and over time I expected him to take some of the load from me, but I still needed to train him more, and I still had to handle any problem that arose, to make sure there was enough money to pay everything that needed to be paid and to make the decision about whether to buy a second studio or expand this one.

I rushed home, showered and changed, and hurried out again. This time of day it took almost an hour to drive to Boston. I didn't want to be late. I parked in the lot outside Terminal E and checked my makeup in the rearview mirror. I was more nervous than I'd been in a long time. My hands were shaking. I took a deep breath to calm myself, got out and went inside to the lower level, where passengers arrived. People were already coming out from customs. I feared I'd missed him.

I was about to turn and see if he was already in the terminal when the doors opened again and Mimmo walked through. It was a strange feeling, as though I was seeing him not just with my eyes but with my heart. For an instant I couldn't breathe, I couldn't speak, I couldn't move. We'd been apart for two and a half months, during which I'd changed so much. Not physically, but mentally and spiritually. The darkness had begun to allow in some light. I had a life. I wanted to have a life. I knew it was okay.

I was trembling as I started toward him. He scanned the terminal and saw me. His face lit up. Instantly he began toward me, at first walking, but then breaking into a quick run. I ran to meet him. We came together and embraced as though we were long lost lovers who'd known each other for a lifetime and had been torn apart, finally to be reunited.

I held his body, feeling his strength and confidence and desire for me. He'd been on a plane all day, but he smelled so good I didn't want to let go. His arms wrapped tightly around me. I didn't want him ever to let go of me either. I felt his breath on my neck.

"It's so good to see you, Luisa," he whispered. "I missed you so much."

I'd been scared to say it first. "I missed you," I said. "I'm so glad you're here."

People rushed past us to catch taxis or meet the people waiting for them. We held each other for a long moment and then, holding hands and staring into each other's eyes, we walked toward my SUV in the parking lot, both of us eager to see exactly where it would take us.

For more about the author please visit:

www.luisacloutier.com

www.untilforever.net

www.facebook.com/luisacloutierauthor

View other Black Rose Writing titles at www.blackrosewriting.com/books and use promo code **PRINT** to receive a **20% discount** when purchasing.

BLACK ROSE writing™

CPSIA information can be obtained
at www.ICGtesting.com
Printed in the USA
FFOW01n2232100418
46227013-47568FF